Hydroponics Garden Secret

A BEGINNER'S GUIDE ON HOW TO BUILD AND MAINTAIN A HYDROPONICS SYSTEM. LET'S DISCOVER TOGETHER ALL THE SECRETS OF GARDENING IN WATER

Richard Garden

Hydroponics Garden Secret

Table of Contents

Hydroponics Garden Secret

Hydroponics Garden Secret

Introduction

Hydroponics can be depicted by just saying that it is a procedure of developing plants with water and supplements without the utilization of soil. The water is given to the underlying foundations of the plants that are being developed. The plant roots may hang in the supplement arrangement, clouded, encased within a holder, or a trough that is loaded up with a dirt substitute. The substitute can comprise materials like sand, perlite, sawdust, stones, wood chips, or rock wool. Any substitute being utilized should give extraordinary water holding capacities yet be permeable enough for gas trade. Between watering the plants, it will end up being a capacity zone for water and supplements for the root framework. The plant establishes development in the substitute to make sure about the plant inside the holder or the trough.

Water is the fundamental element of all life, and it has a particularly important job in the life of plants. Tragically, the dirt and condition that plants, for the most part, develop in are a long way from great. In this manner, the objective of hydroponics is to attempt to reproduce what happens in a completely regular and ideal developing setting. This is accomplished by reliably enhancing the water with supplements, and afterward making these accessible for ingestion by our plants. We allude to this water as a fair 'supplement arrangement.'

The supplement arrangement that you will gracefully is commonly given through a human-made installed framework. This offers to ascend to the advantage of staying away from the vanishing that happens in soil. We're guaranteeing that this supplement rich water is consistently accessible to our plants when they require it. Regardless of whether you know it or not, you've likely previously rehearsed basic hydroponics by placing blossoms in a container and including an instant supplement arrangement.

Hydroponics is reliably developing in fame in the cutting-edge world, from lawn dares to hydroponic applications on space stations! Hydroponics will assume an essential job in having the option to give sustenance as people keep on investigating the chance of living on different planets. On an increasingly superior level, hydroponics offers a moderate method for delivering nourishment for low-pay regions of the world and the prominence of developing hydroponically as a leisure activity has increased a reasonable arrangement of prevalence over late decades.

An extraordinary method to depict hydroponic cultivating is to state that it is a dirt-free sort of planting. Extraordinary jumps in innovation have permitted plants to develop without soil. In any case, this remarkable method of planting that is quickly turning out to be mainstream has been around for a considerable length of time.

This is the Hanging Gardens of Babylon. These new types of hydroponic planting were put on ziggurats, which were watered through partitioning channels, and provided with water from the Euphrates River.

Old Mexico additionally had its form of hydroponic planting. Coasting gardens, or chinampas, are gardens with plants developed in a lake in old Mexico.

Be that as it may, a definitive beginning of hydroponic planting happens in nature itself. No human obstruction or structures occurred in this normally delivered hydroponic nursery.

Hydroponics Garden Secret

For instance, orchids are the hugest instances of hydroponic cultivating. They have aeronautical roots that intrinsically needn't bother with soil to flourish.

Hydroponics is viewed as the following stage in the development of horticulture by numerous specialists as it has upset the capacity to develop plants and yields. It is frequently utilized in nurseries to explore different avenues regarding and develop various assortments of plants. Hydroponics is progressive since it wipes out the requirement for what was viewed as a significant component for developing plants and harvests, to be specific soil.

There are three parts that plants require to develop accurately i.e., water, air (oxygen and carbon dioxide), and soil.

The rule behind hydroponics is that dirt gives the mineral supplements required by plants just as the secure medium in which they "grapple" their underlying foundations. In any case, it has been found that plants can assimilate the minerals and supplements required for legitimate development from fluid medium and arrangements.

Hydroponics is turning into a broadly acknowledged method for developing healthy and nutritious vegetables, organic products, and blossoms both indoor and outside. It likewise gives us the most powerful yields containing the highest number of nutrients, minerals, and supplements and that too in base space. Today, numerous ranchers overall are utilizing hydroponics for delivering natural products, vegetables, and blossoms in the light of the strategy's capacity to create rich supplements and minerals and exceptional returns. Numerous ranchers are asserting that their creation limit has expanded many-overlap in the wake of utilizing hydroponics.

Hydroponics Garden Secret

Chapter 1: What is Hydroponics Gardening?

A variety of practices of farming have been arising to increase productivity. But all these farming practices have remained focused on the land as a medium for increased productivity. For example, two of the known practices employed for extracting maximum yield from the land of agriculture are extensive and intensive farming.

The first farming practice is Intensive farming that uses special techniques of agriculture and higher inputs to improve total yield. An agricultural method in which labor and resources are used at a high degree as compared to the area of land. In a densely populated region, it is practiced. The landholding is small and expensive. Farmland is close to the market, and per hectare output is significant.

On the contrary, Extensive Farming includes the acquisition and usage of more land under cultivation for increased productivity. Extensive Farming involves cultivation on large farms with lower inputs relatively, that is, labor and capital. It is a technique in which the cultivation of large farms is done, with lower inputs relatively, i.e., labor and capital. In a medium populated region, it is practiced. The landholding is comparatively inexpensive and large. Farmland is located in a remote area, and per hectare is small the output is.

The primary emphasis of intensively farming is on the amount of the harvest produced, whereas extensive farming influences quality. Moreover, intensive farming causes harm to the environment, as there is excessive use of chemicals that not only decreases the fertility of the soil but also contaminates the nutrition, which is not in the situation of extensive farming.

Productivity-Centric Farming Methods and Hydroponics

Agriculture, in the past century, has been characterized by increased productivity. The agriculture industry has witnessed the substitution of synthetic fertilizers and pesticides for labor, farm-subsidies, water pollution, etc. The applications of scientific study since 1950 in agriculture comprise gene manipulation, hydroponics, and the development of economically viable biofuels like ethanol.

Hydroponics- An Overview

In contrast to the above-mentioned farming systems used for maximization of productivity, hydroponics is the farming or growing system in which plants are grown in an artificially- controlled environment without using soil. Hydroponic is composed of two roots. "Hydro," the first root is from English, and it refers to water. "Ponics" is the second root that has been borrowed from the Greek, meaning, "toil, to labor."In fact, "Ponos" is a variation of "Geoponics," the science of agriculture.

The term hydroponics is defined as the process of growing plants without soil. It is also described as a process of cultivation of plants in nutrient solutions with or without an inert medium (such as soil). The nutrients solution provides mechanical support to the plant.

Over a soil-based growing surrounding, many distinct benefits are offered by Hydroponics.

- Hydroponic plants grow abundantly and quickly.
- This hydroponic system makes use of resources efficiently.
- It saves space and water. Hydroponics eliminates many problems with soil such as insects, diseases, and poor quality.
- It needs fewer chemical inputs such as pesticides, herbicides, and fungicides.
- It's clean and cool.
- It is characterized by automatic feeding with no weeding.
- Compared to a traditional soil environment, a hydroponic developing surrounding provides the grower an extraordinary level of authority over the cultivation process.
- The hydroponic system enables the grower to precisely control the composition and amount of the nutrients which have access to the plants.
- This system lets the grower control the pH level of the growing environment and protects plants from pollutants and pest's exposure.
- In a hydroponic system, it is easy to recycle irrigation water. Moreover, in the hydroponic method water more efficiently can be used.
- Plants that are grown hydroponically develop faster than soil developed plants. This is because nutrients and oxygen are intensively and directly delivered to the plant's root.

The hydroponic system fosters rapid plant growth which results in fewer times till it is harvest. This, in turn, facilitates the fitting of more cycles of growth in a given period. Since finding nutrients is not that much hard for plants so they can spend more energy in the development of vegetables and fruits, so plants also generally have higher yields in hydroponic systems.

Additionally, anywhere plants set up can be done because hydroponic systems don't depend on external conditions. It is right even plants have an inhospitable external environment. In contrast to soil growing environments, the hydroponic method provides the use of space more efficiently. For urban environments areas with small cultivable soil and where tight space is present, the hydroponic system is especially well-suited for use. Furthermore, artificial light usage in indoor environments can help in making hydroponic growth feasible in areas where sunlight exposure is problematic, due to the surrounding climate or seasonal conditions.

However, it requires specialized skills and significant financial investment on the part of the grower. Hydroponics is a significant disadvantage in the area of cost. The essential initial cost of the hydroponic method set up is higher than a similar soil-growing plant system set up. The hydroponic method is also labor-intensive. Therefore, there are relatively high maintenance costs for the hydroponic method. Hydroponic system some cost can be balanced by the efficiency of the system in using soil, fertilizers, pesticides, and water.

Hydroponics is Soilless Growing

No soil is needed for a hydroponic system. Isn't it remarkable! We are so used to growing plants in fields and gardens that we consider something else completely amazing. Still, that's true. Plants not only thrive without soil but also thrive much improved with their roots in water or very humid air instead. Growing, soilless plants is known as hydroponics. This may sound odd, but several foods we eat — Including tomatoes on the vine — have grown hydroponically.

Now let's look at hydroponics more closely, to find out how does it work!

Plants, as we all know, grow through a process called photosynthesis.

For respiration, reproduction, and growth plants need food. Plants prepare their food by photosynthesis method.

Photosynthesis occurs in chloroplasts. These have chlorophyll in them.

For the process of photosynthesis, plants require to take in the groundwater, from the air CO_2 (carbon dioxide), and the light of the sun mostly. In this process, the plants convert water and CO_2 into glucose (plant energy source) and oxygen (released in the air as a waste product) and. The following chemical equation describes this process:

$$6CO_2 + 6H_2O \rightarrow C_6H_{12}O_6 + 6O_2$$

You can see that this equation does not contain soil as an agent or ingredient, and this validates the fact that plants can be grown without soil. Plants only need water and nutrients, which can be easily obtained from the soil. However, plants can get these things by standing with their roots in nutrient-rich solutions thus enabling them to grow without soil altogether. This is the basic principle behind hydroponics. The word "hydroponics," in theory, means growing plants in water (from two Greek words meaning "water" and "toil"). Still, because you can make them grow without actually erect them in water, most people define the word to define growing plants without using soil.

Hydroponics' Advantages over Soil Growing

Generally, a hydroponic growing system is a system in which plants are grown-up in an artificially regulated soilless environment, which provides many different advantages over a growing environment dependent upon soil. Hydroponic plants grow rapidly and abundantly, and hydroponic systems also allow successful resource use. Hydroponic systems, however, require the farmer to have specialized skills and substantial financial investment. This fact shall keep the space open for conventional, soil-based agricultural operations.

The hydroponic methods for their best yields are known and the consistency of their products' quality. Plants obtain the nutrients they need in a well-designed and productive system and more efficiently consume nutrients than soil-grown plants. To plant roots directly nutrients are added, so plants do not require further use of energy looking for nutrients and water while establishing an extensive root system. More oxygen is available to the plants, which results in faster growth than they do when they are cultivated in soil. Besides, because of the smaller root system, more plants can be grown in less space without

13

thinking about the plants fighting with themselves for nutrients and water.

Hydroponics Provides Control

A hydroponic growing environment provides the grower with significant control over the cultivation process as opposed to the current soil environment. With hydroponics, the grower can precisely monitor the quantity and conformation of the nutrients that plants have access to; the access of plants to soil nutrients is much more challenging to regulate, and it can be hard to determine the accurate composition of soil nutrients. Besides, hydroponics also allows the farmer to protect plants from contact with pests and contaminants, and control the growing environment's pH level. Water can also be more efficiently used in a hydroponic system, and water irrigation can also be recycled.

Hydroponics Facilitates Faster Growth

Plants grown hydroponically steadily grow faster than the plants grown in soil, as oxygen and nutrients are supplied directly and intensively to the roots of hydroponic plants. The rapid growth contributes to shorter periods before harvest, so more cycles of growth can fit in a given time frame. In hydroponic systems, plants also typically have higher yields because the plants do not have to work hard to discover nutrients and can dedicate more time to fruits and vegetative growth.

Hydroponics Enables Water Conservation

With the increasing In addition to its scarcity, the value of water as a resource, the use of hydroponics, and other water-saving techniques for crop production is now required. It is likely to become common in time. Hydroponics requires even less energy relative to plant agriculture instead of soil farming. Much of the water we provide to the plants is leached deep into the earth, which becomes inaccessible to the roots of the plant. On the other hand, plant roots are either dissolved in water in the hydroponics, or a film of nutrients blended in water always covers the root region, keeping it hydrated and nourished. Through this process, water is not lost, because it is collected, purified, replenished, and reused. The nutrient solution can be used as an alternate water supply under the hydroponic method for seed production (Choiet al., 2012). Hydroponic systems encourage the reduction of irrigation power, nitrogen, and improvement of the production of food and energy relative to conventional farming.

Additionally, through recycling run-off water, NFT-based hydroponics will reduce irrigation water use by 70 percent to 90 percent. Under maintained hydroponic conditions, high-value, good-quality vegetables can be efficiently produced using 85 to 90 percent less water than conventional soil growth. Factors that may impact plant yield and affect plant conditions, including salinity, dissolved solids, and contaminants, are generally present in water supplies from groundwater or dam/river water. Whereas some of these variables help crops, others need to be decreased.

Hydroponics is not Wary of Environmental Factors

Since hydroponic systems are not reliant on environmental conditions, they can be set up practically anywhere, even when the outside atmosphere is inhospitable for plants. Hydroponic systems also use energy more efficiently than growing environments for soil. They are typically suitable for urban environments where there are tight spaces and areas where cultivatable soil is small. Moreover, the artificial light is used in indoor environments that will make hydroponic growth feasible in areas where sunlight exposure is challenging, either due to seasonal conditions or the surrounding climate.

Hydroponics is Comparatively Cost-Intensive

Set-up cost is the one section where hydroponics is at a significant disadvantage to soil-growing. The initial cost of setting up a hydroponic system is much higher than the cost of setting up a similar soil-growing system, and it is labor-intensive to run a hydroponic system. Therefore, there are still reasonably high continuing costs for a hydroponic system. Many of the costs of a hydroponic device can be balanced by the flexibility of the system in using water, nutrients, fertilizers, and pesticides.

Chapter 2:   Hydroponics Gardening vs. Aquaponics

What is Aquaponics

Aquaponic gardening is a system of food production that combines aquaculture and hydroponics. Aquaculture is the process of raising aquatic animals such as fish, prawns, crayfish, or snails in tanks. Hydroponics is the process of cultivating plants in a symbiotic environment, in water.

The different forms of aquaculture include fish farms, Mariculture, algaculture, and integrated multitrophic aquaculture; each one of these systems produces different products and provides different uses. Mariculture is the cultivation of animals or plants that require a saltwater environment. Examples of these types of products include many types of shellfish, finfish, flounder, and sea plants, like seaweed. This type of system is either set up in the ocean, where the environment is already perfect for the organisms, with large nets or tanks put in the ocean water, or tanks outside the ocean filled with saltwater.

Hydroponics Vs Aquaponics

They sound a lot alike, don't they? Hydroponics and Aquaponics? They are similar in one way, but vastly different where it counts. Hydroponics means grown in water. If you take the words aquaculture + hydroponics and put them together, you get aquaponics. Let's look at the two processes in more detail to see why one will be better for you over another.

Ditch the soil. Both systems offer to grow a garden without soil. This represents a considerable benefit. Soil becomes stagnant after years of cultivation, requiring a lot of fertilizer and/or rotation of crops. Merely replacing the soil during repetitive seasons of indoor growth becomes expensive on top of that, the soil is easily contaminated with spores or pests laying eggs, perpetuating all of the diseases from one season to the next. Growing in the soil almost requires an outdoor garden, and living in a climate zone with harsh winters means you can only grow your veggies half of the year. Both systems offer value in growing without soil.

Instead of soil, you'll grow your plants in a biosystem of specially cultured beneficial bacteria, and your very own circle of life will sustain both fish and plants. This healthy substitute for dirt is simple to produce, and you'll wonder why you never tried aquaponic gardening before.

Fertilize the water. Both systems require nutrient-based water for plant growth. Hydroponic gardening employs chemical nutrients, which represent constant overhead. You may obtain your growing medium from any number of suppliers, but let's face it: the uncertain role of chemicals in cancer and congenital disabilities is generating headlines around the world. In aquaponics, you may grow organic vegetables through natural fertilizer produced by fish swimming around the tank. The advantage goes to aquaponics.

Design the right space. Both systems require light and a floor strong enough to withstand some pretty hefty weight. I was clueless. I imagined a sweet little aquarium with plants above it and was shocked to realize a twenty-gallon aquarium weighs a whopping 225 pounds. A concrete floor in the basement sounded smart, but I was hooked on the idea of cute goldfish and had a 14-ft bay window in the dining room, so the scales became my enemy.

Figure about one inch of fish per gallon of water. If I have a fifty-gallon tank, you'll need fifty-one-inch goldfish. As they grow, that number decreases.

My research suggested that I needed at least a fifty-gallon tank, so I had to adjust my weight limits to six hundred pounds. If space and weight are an issue for you, hydroponics has the advantage in this case.

Both systems are going to affect your utility bills. The difference between them is that in hydroponics, the water may not be recycled. In aquaponics, the water must be recycled to formulate the rich growth medium to fertilize the plants. A high-water bill would make it cheaper to buy the produce at the market, which makes aquaponics preferable.

Both require a growth medium that serves as an anchor for the plants, helps regulate temperature, and provides constant nourishment. In aquaponics, hydroton is a popular form made from clay. I wanted to get a product I was accustomed to using, but all of them were on the no-no list: sand, vermiculite, peat moss, wood chips, and pearlite. On the plus side, this represented a one-time purchase, and I could live with that. I

Hydroponics Garden Secret

see no substantial value of one system over the other because both require a mix to hold the plant.

Both systems require an investment in setting up the apparatus. A hydroponic garden is cheaper to start if you employ a wicking or water culture system. Both require a more complicated design for some setups, and hydroponics equals the cost of aquaponics when you add a sump pump and additional piping. Aquaponics requires an investment in fish, but the cost will be less than continually buying chemical fertilizers for the water. In this case, the plus goes to aquaponics.

However, the learning curve is higher for aquaponic gardening. Because you are dealing with live organisms to create the fertilizer for your plants, it takes time and experimentation to get the right mix for ideal growth. If you require instant gratification, go with hydroponics. If you like a challenge, like to putter with details, and are willing to wait for results, go with aquaponics. For ease and learning the plus goes to hydroponics.

To better assess these differences, you first have to have a clear idea of how regular gardens work.

Regular gardening:

- Plants are planted on the soil, which provides growing medium as well as needed nutrients.
- Sunlight and rain provide other needs for photosynthesis.
- Needed nutrients and water may be supplemented by the use of fertilizers and irrigation.
- Hydroponic gardening:
- Plants are placed in an inert medium
- Water is continuously pumped through the root of hydration.

- Nutrients are introduced through specially made chemical mixes dissolved in the water.

This system is often seen as more advantageous compared to regular gardening because of the level of control that can be had on the environment. There is also improved hydration and better control over the available nutrients for the plants.

The chemical mixes can be customized according to the needs of specific plants and their current stage in the growth cycle. This translates to yields that are more consistent and enhanced production.

Aquaponic Gardening:

- **It is the same with the hydroponic system with regards to the nutrition and hydration of plants. The use of chemical mixes may also be implemented to aid plant growth.**
- **Fish and bacteria work together to create much, if not all, of the nutrients needed by the plants.**

Here, you can see that, although relying solely on fish and bacteria might not give you the exact amount of nutrients that you want, aquaponics is also much more economical.

Chapter 3:   Hydroponics Vegetable Gardening List

Vegetable

An extraordinary method to get kids to eat their vegetables is to cause them to develop themselves, only a tip from an individual parent!

Watercress

This is a dull verdant green that is a piece of the kale family. It is ideal for a hydroponic nursery as it adores water. You can develop them from seeds by planting them in pots. This amphibian plant adores marginally antacid water. They should be developed at lower temperatures. Stems from the plant can be cut off and placed into new gaps to start a pristine harvest.

Chives

Chives are handily developed in hydroponic frameworks. It will take between six to about two months for them to turn out to be developed. They can be developed under ordinary conditions. When they have developed, they can be routinely gathered. Daylight is significant for them as they need between 12 to 14 hours every day. They need warm temperatures to flourish.

Kale

This scrumptious plant is an individual from the cabbage family. The best hydroponic framework for this plant is the wicking framework. It is anything but difficult to develop and effortlessly dealt with. Since you are developing it inside, you don't have to stress over utilizing pesticides. Kale can flourish in both warm and cold temperatures.

Lettuce

The model plant for hydroponic development. It is an individual from the daisy family and it is a yearly plant. This is regularly the best decision for learner hydroponic planters. It is excessively simple to develop because they become speedy in a hydroponic framework. You can gather these continually once they arrive at development. You will consistently have a graceful of new lettuce. You can utilize either the Ebb and Flow, aeroponic, or NFT framework. It tends to be developed in cooler temperatures.

Spinach

Start the spinach seeds by developing them in Rockwool. Put the seeds in penetrated gaps and afterward balance simply over the supplement arrangement. An Ebb and Flow framework are best for this. Plants that are growing should be raised a tad to permit oxygen to arrive at their foundations because Rockwool is not an extraordinary conductor. When the seeds have grown, you can move them to a lasting spot. You have to permit around 20 square crawls for each plant. This verdant green is another acceptable plant to develop in a hydroponic framework. This plant improves when it has its underlying foundations lowered in a supplement arrangement that is around five inches down. Since it can flourish in colder temperatures, it doesn't require as much light. You can continually gather this plant for 12 weeks on the off chance that you have the right atmosphere and conditions.

Radishes

Radishes are another simple vegetable to develop hydroponically. You can begin these from seeds, and you should see a few seedlings somewhere in the range of three and seven days. They love cooler temperatures and needn't bother with much light.

Beans

Beans are low support however beneficial. They can be effortlessly developed hydroponically. Lima beans, pinto beans, shaft beans, and green beans would all be able to be developed hydroponically. You are going to require a trellis or something for the vines to develop upon.

25

Sprouting seeds will take somewhere in the range of three and eight days. You can start reaping beans as a rule-following a month and a half. The harvest will keep on delivering for around four months.

Peas

Snow peas like cooler temperatures in the fall and spring. They can't deal with the blistering summer sun. On the off chance that temperatures get more than 86 degrees Fahrenheit, it will cause a reduced case set. Before you plant, you are going to need to pick the sort of peas you are going to plant snap, a day off, English. The English assortment just creates eatable seeds. You can eat both the pod and seed of the snap and snow peas. Peas will be prepared to gather around three weeks after you see blossoms.

Cauliflower

This has a place with a similar family as collards, cabbage, kale, and broccoli. It will have a smaller head that is on average around six inches. It is made of lacking blossom buds. These blossoms are joined to one

26

principle community tail. Having a stable emotionally supportive network is essential to keep everything except for the roots out of the arrangement. You can do this by utilizing a layer of rock where the roots ca despite everything arrives at the arrangement or utilizing a netting that lets the roots develop through it. The supplement arrangement can be conveyed by a dribble framework multiple times day by day. This shields the roots from getting excessively clammy. This is a very financially savvy vegetable since it adores lower temperatures and shouldn't be continually given an arrangement.

Cabbage

You should purchase cabbage seedling to develop in Rockwool 3D squares. When they have become large enough to remain solitary, you can place them in hydroponic pots and spot the 3D square in the developing medium. Cabbage plants need around two feet between everyone for a developing room.

Broccoli

Broccoli has an enormous head that is typically green. The "blooming heads" are orchestrated as branches that sprout out of a thick eatable tail. The head is encircled by leaves simply like cabbage. Most assortments are lasting. You can plant this in May and gather it in the winter or late-winter of the following year. It is an overwhelming plant that should be marked.

Herbs

Herbs are consistently an extraordinary decision to begin hydroponic with, they are commonly simple to plant, will develop fast, spread their smell around the house, and give you incredible fulfillment!

Mint

Mint plants, for example, spearmint and peppermint can without much of a stretch be developed hydroponically. These get utilized as enhancing for refreshments and nourishments for their smell. It is ideal to become these in hydroponic frameworks because their foundations spread quickly. They love hotter temperatures.

Basil

This herb is utilized in numerous culinary dishes. It very well may be developed effectively in a hydroponic framework. Buying a few seedlings at a nursery community and afterward transplanting them into your hydroponic nursery. Ensure you flush all the earth off its foundations before placing them into your framework. They will flourish in either an NFT or a dribble framework. They require a great deal of daylight and need to get around 11 hours day by day. They love warm temperatures.

Thyme

This is an individual from the mint family and is a sweet herb. It will have little pink or lavender blossoms and is ordinarily developed as a fancy, fringe plant, or a herb to be eaten. Thyme should be planted from the get-go in spring. It is a robust plant and develops in many conditions. It prefers full sun and just a modest quantity of preparation.

Tarragon

This is an enduring herb that is utilized for flavoring things like vinegar. Tarragon can develop to around three feet tall and like the moderate sun. It gets a kick out of the chance to have some mutual during the hot piece of the day. Tarragon doesn't have a great deal of aroma while it is developing yet once the tops are gathered, the oil will start discharging its sweet smell.

Sage

This is a bush that is developed for dressings, seasonings, to season meats, and to enhance cheddar and wieners. It tends to be developed from seeds. It should be shielded from the cold and flourishes in full sun. Since the plants can grow three feet in breadth, they should become no under four feet separated. Sage leaves should be reaped before it sprouts and afterward dried on screens in an all-around ventilated room or a dehydrator. You would then be able to store it in an impenetrable holder.

Rosemary

This is a sturdy evergreen bush that is developed for its leaves that are utilized as a flavoring and deliver oil that can be utilized in prescriptions. It will bear light blue blossoms in April or May. The foliage will be wooly and white on the base and gleaming and dull on top. Plants could develop to be six feet tall and keep going for a long time, yet they should be shielded from the virus. They like full sun and essential supplements yet will endure some moderate shade.

Parsley

This is an incredible herb to develop hydroponically. It has an exceptionally long taproot so the holder you put it in should be at any rate 12 inches down.

Oregano

This is a solid enduring that could grow up to two feet tall. It will have a white or pink bloom. Oregano can be developed from seeds or the primary plant partitioned. You can invigorate the foliage by reducing it. You can replant once the plants get woody. This will take around four years. You can utilize the leaves when picked or dry them for some time in the future. Oregano can be utilized to enhance pizzas, spaghetti sauce, or other Italian dishes.

Marjoram

This is a perennial herb that is developed for its flavor. It has been utilized to season meat dishes and dressings. It cherishes the full sun. Since the seeds are amazingly little, it is ideal to develop in pads inside a nursery and once they sprout, you can transplant them once the ice has passed.

Fennel

This is a perpetual plant that will develop to around four feet tall. Their leaves are separated into string-like portions that are light green in shading and look a ton like a dill. It can develop from seeds that were planted in spring and will develop best when in full sun. Plants should be marked once they arrive at 18 inches. Gather when the seeds once they age. The bloom stalks are incredible to eat directly before they bloom. Fennel seeds can be utilized as a topping. The leaves taste a great deal like anise. Stems can be eaten simply like celery. The seeds can be utilized in vegetable dishes and cheddar spreads.

Dill

Dill is an extraordinary expansion to any hydroponic nursery. It develops all the more once it is collected. If you supplant went through plants with new ones about each three or a month will keep you in a consistent flexibly of dill. The smaller assortment will create a bottomless rich of development that will give you a lot of cuttings from one plant.

Chapter 4:   Hydroponics Grow System

Hydroponic systems can be active or passive. The difference lies in the use of electrical components.

While an active hydroponics system is operated with electric water and/or air pump, a passive hydroponics system is free of technical equipment.

The advantages of the active system are also the disadvantages of a passive system:

On the one hand, an air pump enriches the nutrient solution with oxygen, prevents algae growth, and instead promotes plant growth.

A water pump also enables the commissioning of all hydroponic systems. This also includes systems that are considered to be very efficient and profitable.

On the other hand, without electrical equipment, you are independent of power sources and save on acquisition and electricity costs.

Furthermore, a distinction is made between circulating and non-circulating systems. However, this distinction is of secondary importance for hobby gardeners and is therefore only briefly explained.

In some systems, the nutrient solution passes through the system repeatedly - it circulates. A hydroponic system can also be designed so that the nutrient solution only reaches the roots of the plant once - it does not circulate. The latter is practiced primarily in the commercial field.

Hydroponics Garden Secret

Hydroponic systems (system types)

There are six different hydroponic systems. Every Hydroponic system differs in how it provides water, nutrients, and oxygen to the plants.

The six hydroponic systems include:

- **The wick system**
- **The deepwater cultures**
- **The ebb and flow system**
- **The drip system**
- **The nutrient film technique (NFT system)**
- **The aeroponics system**

To better adapt the system properties to the needs of the plants, further system variations emerged from the six system types, such as the Kratky method, Fogponics, or the Dutch Bucket System.

Wick System

Plants were watered with wick thousands of years ago. The wick system originated from traditional wick irrigation and supplies the plants with a wick.

The wick system is passive, easy to build, and suitable for beginners.

The capillary effect (or capillary action) makes it possible for nutrient solutions to rising to the roots.

- **Layout and function**
- **A simple wick system consists of:**
- **A water reservoir**
- **A net pot**

- **A wick**
- **A substrate**

The plant is placed inside a net pot above the water reservoir. The upper end of the wick lies at the roots and the lower end hangs in the nutrient solution.

Due to the capillary effect, the nutrient solution rises to the roots. The substrate fixes the plant in the net pot and can store the nutrient solution.

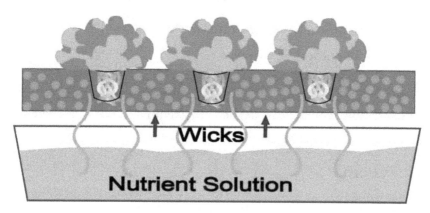

Benefits

- A wick system consists of only four components and does not require a water pump. Furthermore, it requires little maintenance and can also be built on a small scale, for example in a bottle. It is therefore ideal for people who want to gain their first experience with hydroponics.
- Low cost
- Lower expense
- Suitable for beginners

Disadvantage

- Wick's portability is limited. Compared to other hydroponic systems, a wick system supplies the plants comparatively inefficiently. This is also noticeable in plant growth. Likewise, the selection of suitable plants is smaller than with other systems.
- Comparatively inefficient
- Comparatively low yield
- A smaller selection of suitable plants

Plants

Small green-leaved plants, such as herbs, are best suited. However, the herbs should not be too thirsty. For thirsty plants, a thicker or additional wick may have to be used.

Deep Water Culture

If you are searching for a simple and efficient hydroponics system, the deep-water culture is just right for you.

The deep-water culture is passive, easy to build, and very profitable.

The roots always hang in the nutrient solution. The plants have optimal access to water and nutrients at all times. Despite the simple design, this is noticeable in growth.

Layout and function

The plants are placed inside a net pot on a floating platform (e.g. styrofoam). The roots are constantly hanging in the nutrient solution. This is usually enriched with oxygen by an air pump.

A simple deep-water culture of hydroponics consists of:

- A water reservoir
- A few net pots
- A substrate
- A lid for the reservoir

The net pots filled with the substrate are in the lid of the water reservoir. The reservoir is filled with the nutrient solution to the bottom of the mesh pots so that the roots hang in the nutrient solution.

The roots are therefore constantly supplied with water and nutrients.

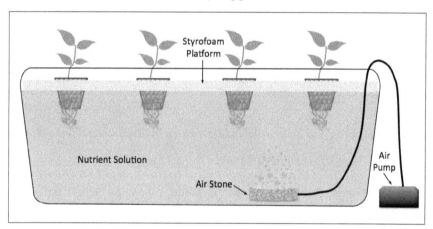

Benefits

- Deep-water culture is the simplest hydroponic system that combines the advantages of hydroponics. Despite the simple construction, very high yields are possible. The low acquisition costs and the low maintenance effort are particularly noteworthy.

- **High yields**

- **Low maintenance**

- Low cost

- Simple construction

- Suitable for both beginners and professionals

Disadvantage

- Because the hydroponics system is not actively operated, there can be a lack of oxygen in the nutrient solution. The result is algae growth and rotted roots.

- An air pump with air stones can help enrich the nutrient solution with oxygen.

- Lack of oxygen

Plants

Leafy vegetables with a low oxygen requirement are best suited for a deep-water culture. However, flowering plants and fruit vegetables can also be reared. In contrast, deep-rooted plants are less suitable.

Ebb and Flow System

Low and high tides not only let the Wadden Sea flourish but also plants in the low and high tide system of hydroponics.

The Ebb And Flow / Flood And Drain System Are An Active, Circulating, And Profitable Hydroponic System.

As the name suggests, the roots of a plant are repeatedly washed with nutrient solution. This makes it possible to adapt the irrigation to the plant optimally.

Layout and function

A basic ebb and flow system of hydroponics consists of:

- **A water reservoir**
- **A plant container**
- **A water pump**
- **A timer**
- **A substrate**

The water reservoir is the tank for the nutrient solution. The plant container stands above the reservoir. This is filled to the brim with a substrate that fixes the plants.

At a specified time, a water pump pumps the nutrient solution up into the plant container. It flows around the roots and floods the substrate and water and nutrients run back into the water reservoir via a small drain.

The water pump is controlled by a timer so that the entire process happens automatically.

Ebb And Flow

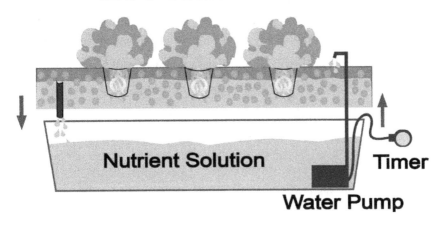

Benefits

- The special thing about an ebb and flow system is the control of the irrigation intensity and thus over wet, dry, or wet periods. Plants from dry regions can also thrive in this hydroponic system.

- Efficient

- Very profitable

- Suitable for plants from dry regions

Disadvantage

- Some experience is required to adapt the irrigation cycle to the plant. Furthermore, the hydroponics system is dependent on a power source.

- Not suitable for beginners

- Moderate maintenance effort

Plants

In a hydroponic ebb and flow system, plants can grow from dry and humid climates. Large, flowering plants such as tomatoes and cucumbers can also thrive. Mediterranean herbs are also often planted.

Drip System

The drip irrigation system, originally from Israel, is also used in the drip system of hydroponics.

The drip system is an active and efficient hydroponic system, which is often used in commercial hydroponics.

As the name suggests, the plant is supplied drop by drop with nutrient solution. The irrigation interval can be ideally adapted to individual plants.

A drip system is often designed as a non-circulating hydroponic system.

Layout and function

A simple drip system in hydroponics consists of:

- **A plant container**
- **A water reservoir**
- **A few net pots**
- **A water pump**
- **A drain**
- **A substrate**
- **A hose for drip irrigation**

In the case of a circulating hydroponic drip system, the plant container with the net pots is placed over the water reservoir.

The water pump continuously pumps the nutrient solution through the hose. The nutrient solution is directed to each plant.

Excess water and nutrients collect in the plant container and flow back into the water reservoir.

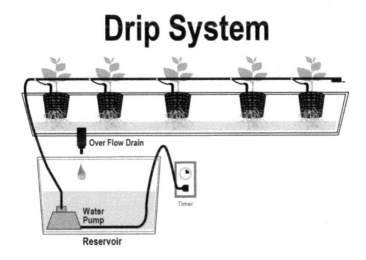

Benefits

- **The hydroponics system is very efficient due to its direct and meterable supply. Also, the hose can be expanded and additional plants can be connected. Compared to other hydroponic systems, a drip system has the best control over the supply of nutrients and water.**

- **Efficient**

- **Scalable**

- Suitable for many plants

- Supply can be adapted to individual plants

- Optimal control over the water and nutrient supply

Disadvantage

- To set and build up the drip irrigation with the nozzles and hoses, a little tact is required. Furthermore, the nozzles can clog and thus increase the maintenance effort.

- Increased acquisition costs

- Mineral deposits can clog drip nozzles

Plants

Because the irrigation intensity can be adjusted individually and therefore the roots are not surrounded by water, all plants can grow in a hydroponic drip system.

Nutrient Film Technique

The nutrient film technique is an active, efficient, and popular hydroponic system.

As the name suggests a thin film of water and nutrients flows along with the roots. The roots are supplied with fresh nutrient solution and oxygen.

The hydroponics system can be designed to be circulating and non-circulating. However, the latter is rare and relatively wasteful.

Layout and Function

A simple NFT system consists of:

- A water reservoir
- A pipe
- A substrate
- A water pump
- Net pots

The net pots with the plants and the substrate are placed in the tube with holes. This is slightly inclined so that the nutrient solution runs through the tube and down into the water reservoir.

Before that, the water pump pumps the nutrient solution to the upper end of the pipe construction. The pumping power and the inclination of the pipe are important. Both should be set so that a thin film of nutrients runs down the tube.

Nutrient Film Technique

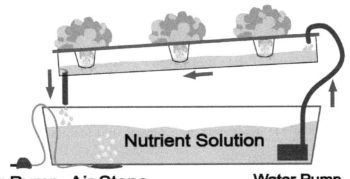

Benefits

- **The NFT system is one of the efficient hydroponic systems. The plants are always optimally supplied with water,** nutrients, and oxygen. It is also a very space-saving system. For example, the pipes can be placed one above the other and thus be installed vertically.

- Efficient

- No / little substrate required

- Perfect for salads and herbs

Disadvantage

- As soon as the water pump stops running, the plants are no longer supplied and can dry out. Another disadvantage is the construction of the hydroponics system. Large plant roots can block the flow of the nutrient solution.

- Short reaction time within the event of a technical defect

- Not suitable for large and heavy plants

Plants

An NFT system is perfect for salads and herbs. Heavy, large, and deep-rooted plants, however, are less suitable. They can put too much strain on the pipe and block it with its roots. In short: green-leaved plants with a short growing season and strawberries grow very well.

Aeroponics

It is probably one of the most modern, unusual, and technically complex hydroponic systems - aeroponics.

An aeroponic system is an active, circulating, and profitable hydroponic system.

The roots hang right in the air and then are sprayed with the nutrient solution via nozzles. This gives you optimal access to water, nutrients, and oxygen.

The hydroponic system is comparatively complex but very profitable and versatile.

Layout and Function

A simple aeroponics system consists of:

- **A water reservoir**
- **Different pipes**
- **Spray nozzles**
- **A substrate**
- **Net pots**

The water pump pumps the nutrient solution through a pipe construction to the spray nozzles. These spray the nutrient solution and thus supply the roots hanging in the air.

The unabsorbed nutrient solution falls back down to the rest of the nutrient solution.

Aeroponics

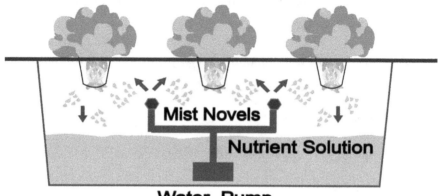

Water Pump

Benefits

- The big advantages of aeroponics are high yields. The roots can develop freely and have optimal access to oxygen. The plants are also in net pots. Therefore, hardly any substrate is needed.

- Efficient

- Little / no substrate necessary

- Outstanding oxygen supply

Disadvantage

- Aeroponics is probably the most expensive and most complex hydroponics system. Nutrients can easily accumulate in the nozzles and hoses and the pipe construction has many individual parts.

- Maintenance

- High acquisition costs

- Short response time within the event of a technical defect

Plants

Due to its supply technology, green-leaved and flowering fruit plants can be grown in aeroponics. However, leafy vegetables and herbs are most commonly grown. Some gardeners even plant potatoes.

Chapter 5: Which Plants Can Be Grown With Hydroponics

The choice of plants is huge because, in principle, we can grow any plant without soil. Therefore, it is completely impossible to list recommended plant species. Therefore, we restrict ourselves to fundamental recommendations.

First of all, we already know that when switching from a soil culture to growing plants without soil, only seedlings should be used. This restriction can be further expanded so that you do not have to experience unpleasant disappointments: we will only transfer plants with a coarse-fiber, strong root system to a culture without soil, that is, plants whose roots when transferred to hydroponics will not receive too serious damage. Among other species, focuses, types of philodendron and monstera, ivy, fatsia, and fatshedera are quite tested to do well.

If we start growing a plant in a soilless culture with seeds or cuttings, then our choice is not limited to anything. Anthurium grows magnificently and gives flowers, which are difficult to find equal in size and color. Species of asparagus are among the most thankful plants for growing without soil. Wax ivy and hoya bloom so abundantly that it is hard to imagine. Focuses usually form 10 to 13 luxurious leaves each year.

This listing could be continued for a long time. So, the author with great success grew, in addition to the mentioned species, indoor lindens, aspidistra, various begonias and ivies, monstera and philodendron, coleus, dracaena and cissus, and, besides, various peperomia and cacti.

For most amateur gardeners, it may be unexpected that cacti can also be grown without soil in nutrient solutions. It is completely unjustifiably widespread that cacti prefer more arid conditions. Anyone who wants to experience special pleasure should conduct experiments with growing cacti on gravel. When our friends get the opportunity of almost unlimited nutrition, that is, they have at their disposal an abundance of water and food, only then they can show how luxurious they can develop. Cacti grown without soil are distinguished by such an abundance and size of thorns as the most precious overseas specimens.

Caring for cacti is not very complicated, but only one provision must be strictly observed: in the winter months, that is, from November to the end of March, watering cacti should practically be stopped. Only every 4 to 6 weeks, the gravel is carefully moistened so that there is no accumulation of excess solution. Cacti cannot be kept in hydroponic vessels.

Here we again have to repeat the demand for the most careful consideration of the individual needs of individual plant species, detailed in many good books on floriculture. They must be provided with such lighting, drinking water, air circulation, and heat, which are favorable for their growth.

A Few More Comments

This sub-heading is based on my practical experience and will be useful for beginners. The so-called calciferous plants - camellias, heathers, and azaleas will grow well only after we take this feature of them into account. Therefore, we must be especially careful in the chemical treatment of the substrate with acid when releasing it from lime and often checking the pH of the nutrient solution. The pH value for these plants is best maintained between 4.7 and 5.8.

Bromeliads can also be grown in vessels and plants without soil, but only in this case, it must be remembered that in this family we deal in most cases with epiphytes, which feed not only with the help of roots. Wild forms of epiphytes live on other plants and feed on leaves. Therefore, these plants always need to fill the inner funnel-shaped leaves with a nutrient solution diluted in the ratio 1: 10 and keep their tenacious roots in a humidified environment. Some of the roots in some species can also absorb nutrients, but on the other hand, we already know that any root system prefers moist conditions.

If you follow these instructions when caring for plants, then Vriesia, Tillandsia, Guzmania, Aregelia, Bilbergia, and all other bromeliads will develop very well.

In conclusion, one more instruction which, without a doubt, can be very enjoyable: in our plants without soils, we can grow banana (Musa). In this case, we are dealing with an exceptionally "gluttonous plant that never has enough nutrition." Since its nitrogen demand is quite high, it is better always to acidify the nutrient solution prepared for bananas with nitric acid, and only in wintertime can sulfuric acid be used as an exception. If we take into account other requirements of the plant - high relative humidity, not too intense exposure to sunlight, and possibly less movement from place to place, then after a year the "plantlets" reached two meters. Therefore, you need to take care of the appropriate size vessel for it.

There is not much left to say about vegetable crops that can be grown in open-air plants and vertical ridges. A standard plant is a tomato that never fails unless mistakes are made too grossly. However, many other types of vegetables will also please us with surprises that you should certainly survive yourself. It is enough to try radishes grown without soil, cucumbers, or kohlrabi to see this.

Far from all plant species have been tested in plants without soil, and anyone who tries to penetrate uncharted areas himself must reckon with possible errors. This, however, does not mean at all that a particular plant was unsuitable for growing in soilless crops. Rather, in this case, we will only be convinced that our first attempt to create conditions suitable for the plant failed. In such a situation, you need to think carefully, look through the special literature, consult with specialists, and try again. Only one thing is unshakable: any green plant can be grown without soil if you know what is required for this.

Work with orchids can be started only by those who already have experience in this field. Whoever does not have such an experience, it is better first to learn how to grow orchids in the same way, and only after that proceeds to grow them in nutrient solutions. Relevant directions can be found in special periodicals and books on the culture of orchids.

Now we have acquired the most important equipment that ensures success in growing plants without soil. Moreover, we visited the past when we considered historical moments and firmly stood with both legs in the present when describing practical experiments. Shouldn't one look into the future?

Hydroponics Garden Secret

Choosing the right site

Humidity

To maintain conditions suitable for plant growth, it is necessary to provide several parameters, the first of which is humidity. In conditions of high humidity, the leaves of plants grow larger. Their maximum growth is observed at 60-80%. But it is better not to stick to the extreme numbers and set the humidity at 65-75%. Cuttings will need more moisture - up to 90%, and 60% is enough for seed germination. During the late flowering, it is best to use minimal humidity to avoid mold.

Humidity is a relative concept: there is much more water in hot air than in cold air. The used percentage humidity parameter is associated with water, which air can hold at a given temperature. This indicator is completely unrelated to the total water content in the air. At ten degrees and 100%, the relative humidity of water in the air will be half as much as at the same humidity, but at 20°C. This means that any increase in temperature in the room will lead to a decrease in humidity.

Ventilation

Ventilation is needed, powerful and reliable, capable of updating all the air in the room in one minute. However, if the fan is too powerful, it will be difficult to ensure constant humidity. You can use an exhaust fan that can replace the air in the room in 4-6 minutes - this is enough, and the atmosphere will be stable in the room.

It is necessary to use different types of ventilation in parallel:

- **An exhaust fan mounted on an outlet in the wall under the ceiling - it will blow air from the room;**

- An outlet with an air intake located on the floor, in the opposite corner to the hood of the room, while the air intake must supply air from the basement or the north wall of the house, it will not interfere with installing a protective net from dust and insects, if this does not interfere with the passage of air;

- Circulation fans will make the air in the room homogeneous, exclude cold or hot abnormal zones, direct them better directly to the stems, which will allow air to be removed from under the crown, making the spread of diseases and insects more difficult.

Carbon Dioxide

The plant feeds on sunlight while consuming the carbon dioxide needed for photosynthesis, during which the carbohydrate necessary for the plant is formed and oxygen is released. This reaction is a source of energy for metabolism and, ultimately, for all life on earth, since plants are food for all life forms, including humans.

But the plant also breathes, while oxygen is absorbed, which, when combined with a carbohydrate, releases carbon dioxide and energy. The plant breathes day and night, absorbing CO_2 for photosynthesis and releasing it when breathing. As a result, more oxygen is released than carbon dioxide, although oxygen is not released at night.

The Optimal Temperature in Hydroponics

The temperature of the air is a very important external factor for the hydroponic plant culture site. This factor largely controls the speed of chemical reactions, enzymatic metabolism, and the development of plants (germination, a transformation of vegetative buds into reproductive buds).

The temperature that the farmer must maintain in his space of culture depends above all on the geographical origin of the cultivated plant. Indeed, these have special requirements in terms of temperature throughout their development: for germination, vegetative growth, floral induction.

Where to place the hydroponic installation?

The best place to place a hydroponic installation is an enclosed space. A basement or a greenhouse is well suited. Also, the hydroponic system can be placed in a small room without windows or in the courtyard of a private house.

The base for the installation of the structure must be strictly even and stable so that the water and the nutrient components present in it are distributed evenly. When installing the structure outdoors, pay attention to the control of liquid evaporation and ensure reliable protection of the hydroponic installation from the wind. Installing the system on the street as a whole is an extremely inconvenient option. Also, you will have to constantly monitor that the hydroponic installation does not cool down, and bring it into the room even with slight decreases in air temperature. In the case of assembling the system in the house, you will have to make more efforts to organize additional lighting. When choosing a suitable place, take into account personal preferences - do as you prefer.

Chapter 6: Water, Nutrient Solutions, and Growing Mediums

Water

Water is the life of a hydroponic system, just like soil is to regular gardening. Not all water is created equal, however, so you can't just carelessly gather from the tap and assume it will work correctly.

Apart from its chemical contents, hydroponic gardeners should also know the density of salts, metals, and minerals of the water. Fortunately, no hard laboratory knowledge is needed to calculate this. There is a device (available in both online and brick and mortar stores) that can measure this, making use of the unit called PPM (parts per million).

If it measures at around 200 to 300 PPM, the water is categorized as soft. Once free of any harmful chemicals, it can be used for a hydroponics system, and without the extra steps needed for its opposite.

Any higher than 300 PPM and that's already categorized as hard water. Hard water is usually rich in magnesium and calcium. Although these two are essential for plant growth, too much will cause deficiencies in the crops instead and will disrupt the balance of the nutrient solution. Therefore, to make it hydroponics-friendly, its mineral content should either be filtered out or diluted with distilled water.

Distilled Water

Since it is free of minerals, it will not disrupt the balance provided by the nutrient solution. Gardeners will be assured their crops will grow or bloom according to their liking.

The problem with distilled water is its neutral pH value since most plants love a more acidic environment. However, this does not mean distilled water should be ruled out from the choices.

pH

The only reason this is a primary topic in hydroponics gardening is that water is more prone to fluctuations and shifts compared to soil. Incorrect pH levels will lead to growth deficiencies; and, should it remain uncorrected, it will lead to death.

The entire process may sound easy, but the reality for beginners may be a little crueler. Since it's difficult to know at first how much or how little to add, everything will have to undergo the tiring process of trial and error. Newbie gardeners would have to measure, then adjust, and then repeat from step one until they reach the ideal pH level. This is necessary unless the gardener uses buffers instead of adjusters.

pH shifts do not stop there, however. Once the plant roots start sipping on their nutrients, the pH will once again fluctuate. And this time, not even the buffers would be able to control it. Therefore, after leaving the system for a day, be sure to measure the water's pH again, and adjust if necessary.

Oxygen

It is common knowledge that plants use carbon dioxide, then release oxygen. This is true, but only for the above-ground parts of the crop.

Water and carbon dioxide are the main food sources of plants. Just like the digestion process in humans, they undergo photosynthesis to convert these two to energy. The resulting materials are sugar and oxygen. As everyone perfectly knows, they release the oxygen back to the atmosphere, then store the sugar and use it to grow. But as already mentioned, this entire process applies only to the leafy parts of the crops.

The roots cannot undergo photosynthesis because they are below the ground. But just like the leafy parts, they need to grow and need the sugars to do so. Since they cannot produce their own, they would have to transport those stored in the leaves.

This is not a problem in traditional gardening because soil (if loosened well enough) contains millions of tiny air pockets. Water, on the other hand, is a different story. If you know the basics of gardening, then you'd know that too much water will drown and thus kill the plants.

This topic may have sparked a little confusion. Hydroponics gardening substitutes soil with water, but water drowns plants, so how does everything work? This is the reason why plant roots are not merely dipped in water and the reason why there are different methods of hydroponic gardening... What you need to grasp at the moment is the roots' need to breathe oxygen, because this knowledge would play an important role in everything that follows.

Nutrient Solution

Plants collect the nutrients they need to grow from the soil, and it may have been apparent to you already that in hydroponics the nutrients are supplied by the water. Water alone doesn't have the 14 nutrients plants require, thus there is the need for nutrient solutions.

The first thing to know about nutrient solutions is that it comes in different ratios. Plants constantly change their requirements as they grow; thus, gardeners can't stick to a single solution throughout. Furthermore, different crops require different nutrient ratios. What will make a tomato crop bloom may not do the same for an orchid.

Nutrient solutions can be bought in hydroponics stores, and their ratios are printed on the bottle's label - the three seemingly random numbers at the bottom (e.g. 2-1-6, 0-5-4, or 5-0-1). Each number stands for the three primary macronutrients, commonly known as NPK or nitrogen (N), phosphorus (P), and potassium (K). Although they are called 'ratios', these numbers are the percentages of each macronutrient against the entire bottle. Therefore, if the label says, 2-1-6, it means it contains 2% nitrogen, 1% phosphorus, and 6% potassium.

Growing Mediums

Rockwool

Rockwool has the fantastic ability to quickly absorb nutrient solution (water), which is why you need to be careful about getting it too saturated to the point that your plants' roots become suffocated. Otherwise, you risk getting root and stem rot.

Composed of granite and limestone, Rockwool is one of the most common mediums for growing hydroponic plants. It can often be bought in the form of sheets, blocks, cubes, and slabs.

Coco coir

One of the best-growing mediums, coco fiber and chips allows sufficient space for the roots and the plant itself to breathe. It also excellently holds moisture and has a neutral level of ph.

Coco coir is organic. But since its decomposition rate is extremely slow, it can break down without having any of its components affecting the chemical composition of your system's nutrient solution. This means that coco coir does not get in the way of your plants being able to grow properly, which is why it is just right for use in hydroponics gardening.

Water-absorbing polymer crystals

Many industries have a use for water-absorbing polymer crystals – this type of hydroponics growing medium is used in making baby diapers, cooling sport cloths for the head and neck, and even soil gardening. Water-absorbing polymer crystals are also used in keeping cut flowers fresh for longer.

River rock

River rock is a type of growing medium that consists of round-shaped and smooth-edged rocks formed by being tumbled down the river. In the case of manufactured river rock, its similar shape and texture as that of natural river rock is a result of letting it run through huge mechanical tumblers.

You can purchase river rock in a wide variety of sizes. They don't cost that much, and you can easily find them in many home improvement centers as well as pet supplies stores.

Gravel

One of the most commonly used and easy to find substrates is gravel. Gravel can frequently be found in the ebb and flow system because of its weight and durability. That benefit, however, is also what makes it problematic. Gravel can be challenging to carry around because it's heavy and can damage plants if you're not careful.

Another pitfall is that gravel is not porous at all and retains no water

Perlite

Perlite is a type of growing medium that is made up of minerals that have undergone extremely high temperatures to make it expand. The heating process turns perlite into an extremely light material that is porous as well as absorbent.

Vermiculite

Similar to perlite, the silicate mineral vermiculite also expands when it is subjected to extremely high heat. As vermiculite is extremely light, you might want to avoid using it in an ebb-flow hydroponics system, where it will tend to float.

Sand

A commonly used growing media in growing hydroponic herbs and vegetables, sand, is similar to a rock. But since it is considerably smaller than regular stones, it does a better job of retaining moisture.

Pine bark (composted and aged)

This type of growing medium is among those first used in hydroponics gardening. Pine bark used to be thought of as a waste product; later on, it is useful in mulching garden soil as well as in serving as an active substrate for some hydroponically-grown fruits, vegetables, and herbs.

Rice hulls

Rice hulls are byproducts of rice production. They are commonly classified as aged, fresh, parboiled, composted, or carbonized. Although rice hulls are organic, they have their use in hydroponic gardening as a type of growing medium since they tend to decompose at a very slow rate (similar to that of coco coir).

Grow rock (hydro corn)

Grow rock (hydro corn) is a form of clay. This clay aggregate has undergone a super-firing process that leaves it porous, lightweight, and expanded.

What is great about using grow rock as a hydroponics growing medium is that, although it is considerably light, it is still heavy enough to avoid floating in your system.

Grow stone hydroponic substrate

While grow rocks are made of clay and are shaped like marbles, grow stone hydroponic substrate is made from glass that has undergone the recycling process and is unevenly shaped.

Growstones are remarkable in their ability to effectively wick up nutrient solution up to a height of four inches above your hydroponic system's water line.

Oasis cubes

Oasis cubes share the same cube shapes and absorbent properties as Rockwool cubes, although oasis cubes work more like floral foams, which are usually used by florists to display their stemmed flowers.

Due to their open-cell structure, oasis cubes can effectively absorb water as well as air. Moisture is wicked by the open cells throughout this growing medium, making it easy for your plants' roots to grow and expand throughout.

Coconut fiber

This is an organic material that is great for this kind of growth. It can hold air and water perfectly and has the bonus of being able to protect the plants from fungus. There are several different names that this comes under so you should look around for it. You will find it as a compressed block that will expand as soon as you place it into some water.

Chapter 7:   Hydroponics Garden Secrets

Choosing The Right Type Of Crop

In the technique of the hydroponic system, almost every plant can grow, but as a beginner, you can start with small plants by which you gain knowledge and experience.

The first step is, choose those plants which need less maintenance and nutrients. As a beginner, you can take herbs and vegetables. Therefore, growing small plants can improve your experience as well as learn new things which are best for the future when you produce other plants.

Make A Proper Plan

When you make up your mind to plant a specific type of crop in your hydroponic garden, the next step comes is planning. Means knowing varied kind of nutrients which are essential for plant, various equipment, photoperiod, etc. so that you have a full overview of how it can offer better results.

Make a list of every small to the massive thing before planting a crop.

Why and when to test and adjust the ph level in hydroponic plants

Every plant which you plant in your hydroponic garden only absorbs nutrient solution in the PH if the answer is in between the range of plant which you have planted. However, if the Ph is not up to the mark, then it won't matter how much your nutrient solution is, the plants will suffer from malnutrition and will die after some time.

For beginners, it is recommended that they will check the PH of the plants daily for the best results.

67

Have Proper And Sufficient Lighting

When you search the market, you will get countless types of grow lights according to your budget. To offer the right kind of lighting to the plants, you have to gain knowledge on that which depends upon the space, the overall distance between the plants, and most crucially the budget.

The types of lighting are: -

- **High-Intensity Discharge (HID) is suitable for extensive hydroponic gardens that have virtuous airflow and proper vent.**
- **Compact Fluorescent Lights (CFL) offer good results in small rooms.**
- **Light Emitting Lights (LED) are also best for small hydroponic gardening but they are more expensive than CFLs.**
- **Whatever, you opt for, to ensure that it will discharge light within 400 and 700 nanometres.**

Having Control On Temperature

This is one of the essential tips of hydroponic gardening. If the temperature of the plant exceeds 85 degrees, the overall growth of the plants will stop quickly. If the gardener is using HID lights, then it becomes challenging to control the temperature.

For maintaining the accurate temperature, the gardener has to install centrifugal fans, but in some cases, the fans alone cannot solve the problem.

For this, plan hydroponic gardening when the outside temperature is 55 degrees or less. Therefore, it is possible to pull fresh air into the garden. On the other hand, you can install air conditioning.

The Right Type Of Equipment

First and foremost, one thing which you need to consider before setting up a system of the hydroponic garden is to have proper and unique tools. Like- dark area, hydroponic gardening system, an oscillating fan, TDS meter, maybe an air conditioner, a digital timer, etc.

Select An Appropriate Nutrient

You have to gain knowledge with regards to varied nutrients which are crucial for plant growth when you start gardening. Side by side, an individual must know about the number of nutrients required by diverse plants or which plant you have grown.

However, timely purchase the adequate and right equipment to check the nutrient level of the plants as per the requirement.

The Health Of The Roots

The health of the root is essential for the overall growth of the plant. From time to time check the origins of the crop so that plants will not suffer from any damage. While offering nutrients to the plants minimizes the amount of light so that algae and fungus will not damage the roots of the crops.

Offering Water To The Plants

This tip is one of the crucial ones because overwatering the plants will damage the crops. In reality, the water intake of the plants depends upon the type of plants means whether it is small or large.

Crops that grow in the dry season need more water than crops that grow in a humid climate. On the other hand, some plants hold moisture for a long time as compared to other plants. So, while planting a crop see

69

whether it needs more water or less so that you can set up the water draining system.

Maintain The Humidity Level

Varied plants have a different level of humidity on which they can survive on their development. So, keep in mind that plants will grow faster and yield higher crops when they are given the proper level of humidity.

Airflow And Ventilation Should Be Proper

For the healthy growth of crops, airflow is a very vital part that also aids in maintaining the overall temperature of the plants. Fans and air conditioners should be installed in appropriate areas so that plants will be healthy.

Understand pH First

The understanding of PH level in plants is must get successful in hydroponic gardening. Interestingly, some meters can take the Ph readings, but on your side, you also have to understand this. The main reason for checking the PH level of plants is that water doesn't have a proper range of Ph by which plants can die or suffer from malnutrition.

Make Liberal Use Of Your Pruning Shears

Any time of the day when you see something on the plant just prune it away, it can rot the full plant. The cleaner you keep your plant higher the yield.

Think About The Taste Of The Fruits Or Vegetables

In this regard, which fruit or vegetable tastes excellent when it is purchased from the market or plucked from the hydroponic garden?

The main motive for doing this is there is an end number of crops that don't have a different taste. Either they are purchased from the market or plucked from the garden. Before deciding to choose the crop to plant give priority to those fruits or vegetables that taste better when they are freshly harvested from the garden.

Take Care Of Space And Type Of Hydroponic System

Well, it is fascinating to grow crops such as corns, melons, and squash, etc but the point is they need ample space. Make sure that you choose the right system and appropriate hydroponic kits. There are countless factors like ventilation, water, etc are crucial elements that make the hydroponic system successful.

Always plant fastest-growing, most natural cultivation, and most crucially which offer high yield

In this field, you have learned as much as you can depending upon your capability. This is the only way by which you can decide which is the right crop for your hydroponic system? Find out the seeds which are cheap and yield high so that your profit margin is also high.

Explore Vitamins B

Many beginners in hydroponic gardening ignore the impact of stress on the plants. If you see that your plants are not suffering from any of the diseases then also, they can face stress issues. So, if you think that your plants are facing stress issues offer them vitamin B supplements that are safe, and with that growth will surge significantly.

The above tips are basic ones, especially for beginners who say that hydroponic gardening is complicated.

Chapter 8: Must-Have Tools

Whether you are about to start your gardening or you had a garden before, this section will be significant for you. There is a lot of experience and information needed to be able to take care of your indoor crops during gardening. Also, all kinds of gardeners will need these helpful tools so that they can get their job done.

This section does not refer to all those fancy pH tools or those high-frequency bulbs or the timers that are computerized and reservoirs. What is being discussed here is the tools that you will be using daily for the daily running of this hydroponic system.

These tools are usually made for gardening hobbies and the traditional act of hydroponics, and they will help your work to be done faster and easier. With these tools, you can rest assured that you will have a better harvest.

Shears and scissors

In the hydroponic settings, you will have to make cuts that are quite precise and are done with very careful clips; this way, your plants will appear more healthy in growth and harvest. And even if you are harvesting from a live plant, or you are just prepping a clone or trimming the excess leave, you will always need to see the use and application of scissors.

When you are selecting the type of scissors to purchase, you should factor in the density of the foliage and also the heartiness of the vegetation; this is needed because cutting off any essential part of the plant will lead to the death of the plant itself. You also have to be precise in the cut.

Also, you should be aware that ragged cutting will not heal fast, and this can affect the productivity of the plant. If the scissors are too big, then it will be difficult for you to maneuver the scissors among the leaves and cut off the part that needs to be cut. Hence you should consider buying scissors of different sizes to fit into the particular need that you want to use.

Spray Bottles

As soon as you begin to mix pest control chemicals, you will need to consider the best tools to help you get them out. Fungicides and other chemicals are needed to be applied in sprays, and in a definite concentration, if they exceed their concentration, it can harm the plants. Hence there is a need to have the right spray bottles that can properly disperse the chemicals onto the desired part of the plants.

A lot of the spray bottles have different nozzles that can be adjusted for the desired quantity to come out of them. This means you can switch on the type of chemical quantity that you want to come out of the spray bottle. There are standard spray bottles which are just like the ones you use in the household cleaning, there are also bottles that come with rotating nozzles, and this is used to apply in spaces that are quite difficult to reach with the primary nozzles.

Pressurized bottles are used to make the spray reach areas where the chemicals are continuously needed without continuous hand pumping. The daily bottles are attached to hoses, and they are mixed with the solution that you need while it is being sprayed.

Lastly, you should have a different bottle for every chemical as this is to prevent the chemicals from mixing with the other and then result in undesirable harm to the plant.

Measuring cups

When you run a hydroponic garden, you will need to make some precise measurements, and this happens especially for fertilizer and every other additive you will be preparing for the garden. Several of the nutrients will need you to measure them in milliliters, and no matter how small these measurements are, you will have to make them precisely. You may, however, come across some measurements in teaspoons and sometimes in ounces. Hence you should get some measuring cups that will cover these measurements.

The measuring cups can come in different shape and manner; there is the eyedroppers, syringes, beakers, cups, scoops, and pipette. As soon as you are done measuring, ensure that you properly rinse the cups. Hence you should invest some cash into purchasing several of these cups as they are needed in gardening always. There are some of these cups that you are going to use all the time, while some others are just going to be occasionally.

Buckets

The more significant the hydroponic system you decide to have, the more buckets you will have to buy. Sometimes, buckets can be used as growing pots for the hydroponic system. Some buckets are used to hold harvest, and others can be used for mixing and for waste products. Buckets are also used for water, and sometimes, you will see the need to have buckets that will be used to hold other buckets. And just because you chose to have a hydroponic garden, you will begin to have a lot of buckets now in your life from now on.

Brushes

There will be a need to have some brushes on the farm that will help you grow your hydroponic plants. And there will need to use brushes to make a good cleaning on the grime, and this develops inside the system, buckets, filters, and even trays. The gardening that is indoors sometimes can be messy; the onus will lie on you to keep it clean all the time. The salt build-up and hard water deposits can be a source of bacteria and fungi infestation in your environment, and this can only be addressed when you do some cleaning, and this time with a brush.

All these debris are not challenging to remove with a good brush; all that is required of you is to scrub and rinse. You should also get some brushes that can be used to clean pipes. Also, paintbrushes will be an excellent additive to have to the list of brushes that you have. This soft and brittle paintbrush will be used to spread pollen from a particular plant to another.

All these tools are quite famous, and as far as you need to run a hydroponic farm, then you should do yourself a whole lot of good if you want the farm to succeed. Equip yourself even before you have started your farm.

Essential tools for hydroponics

There are tools needed for your hydroponics farm, and sometimes, we do not get familiar with these tools. One of these tools is the Total Dissolved Solids TDS and also the pH meter; you must know how to use these tools because they are crucial to your understanding you're and have a successful hydroponic farm.

TDS meters

This meter is usually used to measure both the combined organic and inorganic substances that are put in a liquid. The liquid, in this case, is water. While the lab-grade equipment used for measuring the liquid is quite expensive and at the same time very difficult to use, there are a lot of inexpensive TDS meters that have been designed for quick and accurate measurements.

TDS meters are used by the hydroponic gardeners to measure so accurately the conductivity and how pure the water is. Pure water does not conduct electricity efficiently as impure ones. Water only becomes a good conductor when other materials get dissolved in it. This conductivity is well measured by the TDS meter in approximation, and then it is converted and then expressed in parts per million.

When you are about to mix the nutrient solution, the instructions that explain how to mix explains it in parts per million. Hence when you begin with a nutrient you haven't used before, you should be wary about how you mix. You should add a small bit of water, then you stir very well, and then you measure the TDS. Then you keep adding the nutrient until you get to the desired TDS>

When you are done, you should do well to rinse the electrode; this will prevent them from destroying and make the meter last longer for future use.

PH meters

The pH meters, as explained before, is used to measure the acidity of the nutrient in the solution. Plants in the hydroponic system will need to be monitored and better administered their nutrient solution; this will help the plant stay healthy, as an unbalanced pH can burn up the part of the plant that is exposed to the liquid.

When the pH is too high or too low, there will be a problem with absorbing the nutrients. And care ought to be taken because the plant survives in a narrow pH. The pH is measured on a scale of 7, and pure water has a pH of 7.

I have here a pH range of some plants

- **Tomatoes 5.5 to 6.5**
- **Cucumbers 5.8 to 6.0**
- **Lettuce 6.0 to 6.5**

As you can see, the pH range of these plants has a small margin of 0.5; hence, any deviation can cause severe damages to them and can affect their yield.

As soon as you are done mixing your nutrient solution, you will have to check the pH immediately to check if it matches your required range; then, you should adjust the pH to the range necessary. It is easier to use digital pH are quite easy to use, and they give pretty fast and accurate measurements; this is because you do not need to calibrate them after every use.

To properly use a pH meter, you will place the electrode in the nutrient solution for a short moment, and then the pH is displayed on the LCD screen on the meter. As soon as you are done, you must keep the pH meter in the right place. The electrodes should be kept clean and wet at all times. You can also get a particular electrode storage solution used to store electrodes.

The pH is temperature-dependent. Hence you should look for a pH meter that has automatic temperature compensation ATC. The ATC is essential because it helps to regulate the temperature; without this, the pH will give a different reading with different temperatures. And this will affect the accuracy of the pH of your nutrient solution.

Also, manual pH meters will have to be always calibrated before use; if not, they would drift. Ensure that you get the calibration solutions when you are buying a pH meter; try to follow the manufacturer's instructions when you want to calibrate your meter.

You will also need to buy phosphoric acid as this will help to lower the pH when you need to. The potassium hydroxide can be used to raise the pH too to the desired levels. These chemicals are used because they are relatively safe, but then you should use them with caution as they can be dangerous to the plants in higher concentrations.

Some gardeners will like to buy pH meters that are easy to use, and they are available from a lot of different sources.

You will also need a thermometer with you to get accurate temperature control. This is one of the ways to get the right temperature that will aid the survival of the plants you are growing.

You will need goggles and gloves; these will serve as some protective covering for your hands when you work on the hydroponic system. Some chemicals are quite harsh when you use them, and if they touch your skin, it could lead to skin burn. Hence a protective glove will help you stay safe.

Hydroponics Garden Secret

Chapter 9: Common Problems

G rowing plants hydroponically is an art. Because you do not have the same set up as you would with a traditional garden, you are responsible for providing your plants with the light, water, and nutrients that they need to grow. Sometimes, however, our systems do not allow our plants to flourish as we intended. In these cases, the first step is to check for common problems in the system. Once you locate what is wrong, you will be able to fix your hydroponic system so that it grows larger, better harvests.

Troubleshooting Issue #1: The Lighting

Whether you are using natural or artificial lighting, there are a few things to consider in regards to how well your plants are growing.

Natural Lighting

When it comes to natural lighting, you should ask yourself:

- Is the plant getting enough natural light? If you are growing inside, be sure the window that your plant is sitting in gets an adequate amount of light during the day. If you are growing outside, make sure the area your plants are in is not covered by shade too much during the day.
- Are you growing out of season? If the daylight is shorter or the shading is different depending on the time of year, you may want to switch to artificial lighting.
- Should you switch to artificial lighting to speed up the growth of your plant? When you use artificial light, you have more control over growth cycles and you can reap more harvests.

Artificial Lighting

- Are you using the right kind of lights? Most fluorescent lights are not compatible with growing plants. You should be using HID lights.
- How close or far away from the plant is the light? Your light should be no lower than 1 foot away, but no higher than 2 feet. Adjust according to the size of your hydroponics garden. You should also adjust the wattage to a higher number of watts the farther you are from the plant.
- Are my plants getting too hot to grow? The simplest way to see if your plants are too hot (your bulb is too close) is to put your hand just above your plants. If it gets hot, then you need to move the light further away.

Troubleshooting Issue #2: The Growing Climate

If the climate is not right, your plants will not be able to grow. Be sure that you take the specific needs of the plant in mind and adjust the moisture level and temperature accordingly.

- Is the temperature of your growing system between 60 degrees and 90 degrees? You should also make sure that the temperature drops by 10 degrees at night, as this is important for the night/day rhythm of the growing cycle
- Is the air being properly ventilated? The last thing that you want is to have an excess of stale air around your plants. You should install a vent or even a fan so that the leaves are gently stirred around throughout the day and night.

- Is the relative humidity of the growing area between 50 percent and 70 percent? This is considered safest for growing because too much humidity can interfere with growing processes and encourage the growth of mold. Between 50 and 60%, is the most optimal range of humidity, but as much as 70% is acceptable for certain plants.

Troubleshooting Issue #3: The Nutrient System

In regards to the nutrient system, here is what you should ask:

- Is there enough solution in the reservoir? If your pump is sucking any air during the cycles, then it is likely you need to add more nutrient solution to your reservoir.
- Do you have an adequate ratio of water to nutrients? If you think that the concentration of your solution is the problem, discard the entire batch and start over.
- Is the temperature of the reservoir below 85 degrees? Keeping the temperature under 80 is preferred, but under 85 is adequate.
- Is the pH of the nutrient system balanced? Check the pH of your nutrient solution regularly to be sure that your plants are getting what they need. If you need to raise or lower the pH, there are drops that you can buy to do this.

Troubleshooting Issue #4: Pests

It can be hard to pinpoint the reason for pests to show up in your hydroponic garden, especially if you have used sterile buckets and nutrient mixture. However, it does sometimes happen and when it does, you need to use one of the following three options.

Hand-Pick the Bugs Off

If you catch bugs early on, this is the most effective way to get rid of them. Pick the pests off by hand and put them in a container (you can release them or kill them). Do this for a few days until you notice that no bugs are remaining.

Take Advantage of Natural Predators

If you have a screened-in porch, or if you are growing your hydroponic garden outside, you may be able to use bugs to get rid of your pests. Bugs like lacewings and ladybugs have voracious appetites when it comes to "bad" plant bugs like mealybugs and aphids. This is a method that you do not want to use for your indoor setup, but it is extremely effective (and safe) for biological pest control.

Last Resort-Organic Pesticides

If you are like most people, then one of the reasons you are growing hydroponic fruits, vegetables, and herbs is because you do not want dangerous chemicals and pesticides in your fruit. Unless you want to throw away your entire crop because of a bug infestation; however, it may end up being your only option. The first thing that you must do is identify the bugs that are on your plant. Then, look for organic pesticides that will not leave a harmful residue on your crops. Here are a few tips:

- Look for non-toxic pesticides. These are going to be the safest for your plants (and you!).
- Follow the instructions closely. Non-toxic pesticides may take several applications before all of the bugs can be exterminated.

- To prevent the artificial or natural light from harming your plants, spray the pesticides in the evening. This will allow them to dry so your plants do not burn.

- If you do have to use pesticides, be sure to stop spraying at least one week before you harvest the plant. Additionally, wash before you eat.

Identifying Critters

Many things can indicate an oncoming critter infestation, including icky coatings, discoloration, and more. Here are the most common bug signs and how you can get rid of them.

1. Webs- If you see the webs on your plants, then spider mites are a likely culprit. Spider mites are red but very small, so unless you are looking for them or you have a large infestation, they are hard to see. In addition to webs, you will probably notice yellowish-white specks on the leaves of your plant. This is caused by the spider mites sucking out the plant fluids. Eventually, this will turn brown unless you take care of the problem. You may also notice the eggs of spider mites, which are small and round. They are also translucent, with a white to amber color.

   - If you catch the infestation early on, you may be able to get rid of mites by raising the humidity and temperature. Because spider mites prefer dry, cool conditions, doing this may send them packing.

   - If that does not work, consider investing in predator mites. These are the natural enemy of spider mites and you will need to purchase one predator mite for every 100 spider mites that you believe you have.

- If you must resort to using chemicals, be sure that you are purchasing a blend made with Neem Oil. You can also consider using Neem Oil by itself, though it may not be quite as efficient as the pesticide.

2. Wilted, sickly plants- If you have noticed that your plants have almost stopped growing, or that they are sickly or wilted in appearance, aphids may be to blame. If you do not resolve this problem, the plants will turn brown and curl inward. This is because aphids suck the sap out of the leaves and also have saliva that is toxic to plants and often filled with disease. If you inspect the underside of the plant, you will find dense, yellowish areas. These are softer-bodied bugs that are known as aphids.

   - These are a bug that you can hunt and pick off, especially because they often hang out in such dense colonies. They may be on the undersides of leaves, but also the tips. Crush them as you pick them off.
   - Some bugs prey on aphids. Some good choices include green lacewings, ladybugs, and gall midges.
   - Neem oil is also effective against aphids. Find a pesticide that includes this ingredient.

3. The cotton-like substance in crooks of leaves- If you have cotton-like substances on your plant, then it is likely mealybugs. Mealybugs have the appearance of cotton, especially when they group in colonies. Your leaves will become distorted and your plants can become weak, often dying quickly.

   - This is a bug that is particularly difficult to battle using the pick-and-remove method. You may be able to win if you catch the infestation very early, but you will need a great amount of vigilance.

- For biological warfare, introduce a couple of ladybugs into the growing environment. Ladybugs find mealybugs to be a tasty treat!
- Neem oil can be effective, so look for a pesticide with this ingredient. You will likely need several applications to get rid of this pest.

4. Whitish-yellow spots with a metallic sheen- If you have whitish-yellow spots appearing on your plants, then thrips may be to blame. These are small wormy-looking creatures with legs. If you do not get the infestation under control, your plants will eventually turn brittle. Here is how to deal with them:

- To locate the thrips, shake the leaves. Then, pick up the bugs and squish them. In the early stages of an infestation, you will be able to kill them by hand.
- Several bugs can help with biological warfare, including green lacewings, parasitic wasps, and predatory mites.
- You will want to treat these with a specific pesticide if they get too severe.

Chapter 10: Maintaining The System

Water Quality

The consistency of their water source must be checked before it is utilized in a hydroponic framework. The pH tests the water level of corrosive or antacid and is basic for observing utilizing pH meter or pH strips. PH scales run from 0.0 to 14.0; unbiased 7.0, acidic under 7.0, soluble over 7.0. In most hydroponic plants, the pH levels of the producers need their water to be somewhere in the range of 5.5 and 6.5, yet if the pH levels remain the inclination of a cultivator and plant type is resolved. Different supplements are devoured at various levels, which implies that the pH required can vary contingent upon the kind of plant or the existing pattern of the plants.

Whatever plant is developed in a hydroponic framework, a cultivator's water flexibly requires enough EC to help sound plants. EC tests the measures of broke up water salts, in which plants must remain solid with supplement and foundation minerals. EC has an immediate association with the supplements accessible to plants, and consequently, EC testing is huge. Interestingly, cultivators can gauge their EC levels with EC meters so an AC voltage goes through them when placing in the water demonstrating the conductivity of the gas.

The water temperature will be somewhere in the range of 68 and 72 ° F in any hydroponic framework. Producers with a water warmer and a water chiller will hold their water-temperatures. It implies that the water isn't excessively warm or unseasonably cold for the plants.

Will Kachoris, who plans custom hydroponic frameworks for GrowSpan Greenhouse Structures and Hydro Cycle Growing Systems, says,

"Utilizing air circulation and a UV sterilizer will permit cultivators with unfeasible water to relax. This decreases the sickness and builds the oxygen consumed with the goal that plants become quicker .. Foaming frameworks, for example, airstones, help to circulate air through the root zone to keep the roots sound, empowering them to expend supplements without any problem.

A Fertigation System

Fertigation is the strategy by which composts are siphoned into the water system framework. In hydroponic creation, the best possible utilization of fertilizer into the water flexibly is basic, because the plants are developed without soil, depending on the perfect measure of water and supplements to flourish.

Kachoris further underlines why the exact utilization of composts in hydroponic development is so basic, "The dirt typically gives a cradle to salts, acids, and bases applied to the framework, without this regular support, producers must be mindful so as not to stun plants with an overabundance of synthetic."

This can be hard to include the right amounts of compost as the pH levels will consistently be indistinguishable level to the plants from the supplements are joined with their water source so the perfect measure of the supplement is assimilated. It very well may be accomplished rapidly without a creation framework since it implies that the cultivator must be taken care of, mixed, and checked physically, by methods for a test and blunder process until the pH level is correct.

The presentation of a fertigation framework would improve the productivity of the activity. "The plants are increasingly sound and reliably took care of to ideal creation," Kachoris says. "This doesn't evacuate estimating pH levels; it will guarantee better conveyance of the right amount of manure unfailingly, making the procedure smoother. Cultivators ought to in any event once per month, ideally once like clockwork, align their frameworks to guarantee that the right measure of manure is utilized and to see that pH is the place it ought to be.

"Expanding work costs in the farming business have been a significant purpose behind cultivators to mechanize the fertigation program," clarifies Kachoris. "The program will pay for itself in a couple of months, which will proceed for quite a long time which years contrasted with a salaried representative."

The Right Growing Medium

The absence of soil in a hydroponic framework guarantees that the plants ought to be conveyed and urged to flow through the supplement arrangement adequately. The revelation of an incredible developing medium causes the plant's underlying foundations to retain a correct equalization of oxygen and mugginess.

For hydroponic frameworks, the mix of dirt and coconut is regularly utilized as the mix holds oxygen and dampness at the world-class level.

Earth pellets are cheap dirt pellets known for their excellent safeguarding of oxygen and cocoa husks are produced using coconut husks, which are rapidly single, yet expensive in the two districts. In this manner, it is frequently joined with rising rocks to decrease costs.

Rockwool is another structure regularly utilized because it resembles a coconut. This keeps up oxygen and stickiness well and is made in shapes with the goal that plants can undoubtedly be placed in columns. The drawback is that after only one use, it must be tossed out.

Clean The System Regularly

Eventually, it is completely conceivable to make every one of these proposals, yet it won't work if the machine is squalid and dirtied. The day by day cleaning of the hydroponic framework is essential if a powerful activity is to keep the framework liberated from sicknesses and nuisances.

The supplement arrangement store ought to be cleaned after complete cleansing in the entire development room. The cylinder is cleaned, filled part of the way through, and a cheated fading arrangement is utilized for compelling cleaning, which guarantees that the tubing doesn't gather strong materials. Cleaning the repository takes normally 2 to 3 weeks, yet the pace of cleaning relies upon the procedure. Valves can be halted from recording once per week by opening for a couple of moments.

During the time spent cleaning, it is basic to scour the containers down or develop plates to forestall pathogen development. This technique is fast and should be possible with a cleaning arrangement and a 10% dye. A rancher will at that point add the detergent and scour as far as possible of the cycle until they are impeccable. Normally after each period of development or after each reap.

Hydroponics Garden Secret

Further ways are...

- Your fluid arrangement ought to be checked something like at regular intervals for your supplement balance. The pH of the supplement arrangement in your hydroponic framework is tried from multiple points of view. The most affordable approach to check the ph. of the arrangements of the supplement is presumably paper test strips. The most widely recognized route for pastime nursery workers is to utilize fluid pH test units. Computerized meters are the most refined method of the following ph. The computerized pen is the most well-known type of meter.

- The water level ought to be tried no less than at regular intervals in your tub. At the point when you add water to the technique, first lift the water with your supplement arrangement or weaken the fluid and toss it into a spiral the correct supplement balance.

- You must test the plants consistently for development patterns and check whether your plants have been influenced by some bug or sickness and afterward do whatever you can to battle disease or inadequacies right away.

- Once full plants (particularly herbs) are developed, you ought to consider garnish and cutting plants at an opportunity to give the plants new vitality and far and away superior development so that they can be utilized in cooking. Gather any herb, organic product, or vegetable that is developed and completely developed to permit the plant to grow more produce, and you will at that point profit by vinified augmentations to your kitchen.

Hydroponics Garden Secret

- Just be aware of the light degrees of plants that develop of daylight, or in fake light and twist with the goal that you can change abundances, for example, including or taking off-screen garments, or move the framework into an increasingly secured region to harm plants. Likewise, test your supplement levels quickly when the plants are presented to rain to abstain from weakening your liquid sources.
- Start following the framework right now that the siphoning framework starts to guarantee that the siphon works and furnishes the plants with fitting supplements.
- After the three weeks, remember o change the supplement repository.
- Repeat the strategy occasionally to keep the pipe smooth and liberated from harmful development, utilize clean water and hydrogen peroxide. The neatness of the framework will consistently be saved.

At the point when you do these things, you can keep up the framework effectively and see great development and improvement during the procedure.

Significance of keeping up the Hydroponic developing

While natural choices can be found on hydroponic yield, the hydroponic water is ordinarily held as close as conceivable to sterile water. When all is said in done, the repository and the hydroponic framework gives your plants the food and water required for their creation and development. Shockingly, this additionally implies infections and undesirable species can likewise create and flourish in an ideal setting.

The supplement and dampness in hydroponic frameworks are full in microscopic organisms and growths. Microbes are singular living beings that develop and increase at inconceivably quick rates and which can create and flourish surprisingly fast. Additionally, they cannot oppose and protect themselves against critical changes to their biological systems as do plant as single species.

For instance, plants may create protective cells on the outside of the root that are intensely rough or destructive in the dirt. They are customized to bite the dust and go about as assurance for the basic living cells. Microbes have no such limit since they are only a solitary creature and are along these lines not fit for safe cells. It is just a single model, yet a few different models are conceivable, how plants can more readily oppose harm to their condition than microscopic organisms can stand up to.

Tips For Keeping Up The Hydroponics Cultivating Framework Viably

In hydroponics, complete sterility is unimaginable and will make plants bite the dust. Be that as it may, steps can be utilized to make your hydroponic medium as comparable as conceivable to the clean medium without jeopardizing your plants:

Change The Reservoir Water Weekly

You can easily adjust the water of your reservoir sometimes to preserve the sterility of your hydroponic system. Once a week, you must ensure that your nutrients are not lost by dumping long before your plant even has an opportunity to use them, even before bacteria take over. It is also a good idea to clear any adhering bacterial film from the interior of your tank and to clean the container of any pump or air pit surfaces. At these places, bacteria can easily hide, where bacteria can again come out when the freshwater is added once again to begin multiplying.

Use Only Clean, Filtered Water

Many find this the most effective way, but not the easiest or the cheapest way to keep your reservoir clean. To do this, you must buy a filtration system or buy filtered water. While this adds a few additional costs to the system, it will do a lot to protect your hydroponic system against pollution and disease.

Reverse osmosis is by far the best choice because up to 99,999% of your tap water dissolved molecules are eliminated. From the beginning, it's almost sterile. Combine it with frequent reservoir shifts, and you will possibly never have a problem with your hydroponic system's bacterial overgrowth. Once bacteria are more abundant, the tank would have been flushed and filled with fresh filtered water once again.

Chapter 11: Planting, Transplanting, and Caring

Once you have everything planned out for your system and you know what plants you are going to grow, you can start getting things growing. Unlike with traditional gardens, there are some other steps that you will have to go through as well.

Germination

There are different ways that you can germinate. One fun way to do it is to place the seeds of your chosen plant in a wet paper towel. Fold them into the towel and then slide it into a clear, sealable bag. The bag should be placed in a warm, dark place to allow the seeds to germinate. You should make sure that the towel remains wet. Some seeds are going to take longer to germinate than others.

There are also seed starter kits that you can use to grow your seedlings. You can use either of these methods, but the power towel method tends to go easier.

If using the towel method, once it has germinated and has a stem that is about an inch in length, it is now a seedling. What comes next will depend on the type of plant you have.

If the stem seems to be a bit on the frail side, keep the plant in the paper towel, but cut a few small holes in it for the leaves to emerge through them. If the seedling has a stronger stem, keep the roots in the wet towel, but allow the stems to straighten out and begin to produce leaves.

You have to keep an eye on the seedlings because they tend to be fragile at this point.

Transplanting

After the seedling has become strong enough, that can be transplanted into your hydroponic system. In general, after the seedling has produces a couple of true leaves, it can be transplanted. True leaves are the first leaves to be produced. The first couple of leaves are called cotyledons. The true leaves will from after them and are larger and darker.

When you transplant the seedlings, you need to make sure that the growing media is keeping the plants supported and in an upright and stable position. The roots should be fully covered so that they will reach your nutrient mixture.

Helping the Plants to Grow

After you have your plants in your system, you will need to make sure that they receive everything that they need. This means you are going to have to keep an eye on the pH and nutrient solution to make sure that the nutrients and oxygen are at the levels they need to be. You should also make sure that your lighting schedule remains consistent for your plants. The plant's first few weeks in the system are the most crucial. These are the weeks that will make or break the plant.

Even though you don't have your plants planted in the ground, there is something that you have to keep an eye out for. Hydroponically grown plants, even when the system is inside, can face pest problems. If you aren't ready for that possibility, then an infestation could happen which would undo everything you have done. Let's take some time to look at possible pests and how to avoid an infestation.

Whiteflies

These bugs are little, fine white bugs that affection to suck the entirety of the juices from your plant when in their grown-up and sprite stages. At the point when the feed, they discharge a sweet liquid, which is called honeydew, which will make a dirty form, which is a growth that is about as engaging as it might sound. You will in all probability observe the shape before you ever observe the whiteflies.

Contingent upon where your hydroponic framework is set up, you can discharge a parasitic wasp that goes after the sprites of the whitefly. You can likewise be proactive and check the underside of the leaves for their small eggs and scratch them off.

You can likewise hang up clingy traps which will work by baiting the whiteflies and catching the grown-ups that are around the plants. Neem oil splash is an extraordinary common choice for forestalling practically any nuisance. The splash upsets the nuisances' taking care of example and development, which will keep the fairies from turning out to be grown-ups. The significant thing is to ensure you focus on the undersides of your leaves and the stems where the sprites want to group.

Arachnid Mites

This presumably isn't amazing, however, these bugs look like insects, yet they are about the size of a pinhead. Grown-ups go in shading from light green, yellow, or ruddy, yet the fairies will in general be yellow or extremely light green. In contrast to real creepy crawlies, which helps plants by eating different bugs, insect parasites can wind up murdering your plants since they suck out the entirety of the stem's juices. If you see yellow dots on the highest points of your leaves, these are the primary obvious signs that you could be managing creepy-crawly vermin, and you could likewise observe a fine webbing on the shoots and leaves of your plants.

Creepy crawly parasites flourish in dry spots, so if your room's stickiness remains at about half, bug vermin will be less inclined to show up.

You can likewise utilize pyrethrin, which normally happens in chrysanthemums, and natural cultivators affirm it. It will deaden the bug and prevent the arachnid bug from taking care of regardless of where they are a major part of their life stage. Ensure you don't mistake pyrethrin for pyrethroids, which are engineered synthetic concoctions that can hurt oceanic life and could hurt your pets.

On the off chance that you notice that a plant has become invaded with bug parasites, detach it since creepy crawly bugs move to new plants with their webbing.

Aphids

Focused or frail plants will draw in aphids, which are delicate, pear-formed bugs that might be dark, dark, yellow, green, or pink. Some of them will have wings, while others won't. They benefit from the sap in your plants and discharge honeydew, which will draw in ants. Aphids additionally spread viral infection starting with one plant then onto the next.

Plants that are overloaded, similar to those that are given high-nitrogen engineered composts are progressively powerless to aphids. Natural plant nourishments are the best. When drenched with water, aphids will in general tumble off the plants without any problem.

The insecticidal cleanser is an extraordinary method to control aphids, just as different vermin. Aphids are usually found outside, in yards and nurseries, so to get aphids far from your plants, don't bring outside devices into your development room.

Thrips

This is one more plant-juice sucker. Thrips are dark, yellow, or earthy colored, and they frequently show up in groups. They favor blossoms just as their unfertilized buds. Leaves and petals they feed on turn weak and dull. The nursery assortment of thrips will drill gaps into the plant's stem and lay their eggs there.

You can delicately shake the plant stems to work up the thrips. The unhatched eggs look a great deal like a pimple or a spot of paste on the leaves. These can be effectively scratched off and afterward crunched.

Clingy traps are another approach to dispose of grown-up thrips. Potassium salts of unsaturated fats debilitate the defensive shell of the bug.

Thrips don't have that long of a real existence cycle, and just live for two or three weeks, so you will continually need to apply your insecticidal cleanser at a ten-day interim to control the sprites and grown-ups.

Growth Gnats

Growth gnats have an appearance near whiteflies, however, they will in general be a grimy dark within white. The grown-up gnats won't cause any harm, yet the hatchlings, which are little, translucent, pale slimy parasites, will eat up the root arrangement of your plant. The worms will likewise benefit from green growth, and they love living in zones that are wet and dull, particularly around the base of the plants.

Ensure that you utilize a green growth and greenery executioner to clear out your hydroponic arrangement of any green growth that parasites could be pulled in to. Slimy parasites feel weak at the knees over Rockwool; however, it doesn't generally make a difference what developing media you use since you have to ensure that you permit them to dry out after your feed and water to deny these irritations of need dampness.

The grown-ups can likewise be caught by utilizing clingy traps. This will keep them from having the option to lay eggs. You can likewise utilize a mixed shower of pyrethrin, insecticidal cleanser, and neem oil to dispose of the grown-ups.

Ensure that you dispose of any plants that have become plagued with worms. Protecting those plants are almost unimaginable. Remember; bugs lay eggs by the hundreds. Never overlook an issue with bugs.

Your plants are similarly as inclined to sicknesses just as bugs. There are five basic sicknesses that a plant can create.

1. Iron deficiency

Characterized by yellow leaves and green veins. This is often misdiagnosed as other diseases.

2. Powdery mildew

Hydroponics Garden Secret

This will look like a white powder has been sprinkled over your plant's stems and leaves. When left untreated, it can stunt the growth, yellow the tissue, and cause the leaves to fall off.

3. Root rot

When too many pathogens are in the water, the roots can end up rotting. This will cause the plants to yellow and wilt.

4. Downy mildew

Downy mildew appears on the underside of the leaves and looks just like powdery mildew. This also causes the leaves to turn yellow.

5. Gray mold

This will appear as small spots on the leaves and leaves fuzzy gray abrasions and will continue to deteriorate until the plants become mushy and brown.

The good news is, you can prevent these problems. First off, make sure that you wear clean clothes when you are handling your plant. Diseases and pests can "ride" into your growing area. You always want to make sure that you have clean clothes on when you go into your grow room, especially if you have been outside. This even includes shoes that you could have walked around outside in.

Second, make sure that you clean up runoff, spills, and so on. Since most mildew and molds, as well as other diseases, can be caused by too much humidity or water, you will need to make sure that you police the water you use.

Lastly, make sure that you keep your plants clean. Make sure that you clean up any dead plant matter that might appear around your plants.

102

You should also make sure that you prune your plants when you need to get rid of any diseased branches or leaves.

The cleaner you keep your plants, the better off they will be.

Chapter 12: DIY Plans

You don't have to develop your new product is a major nursery. You needn't bother with long periods of experience to make your own Indoor Rising DIY organize. That is the Hydroponics enchant.

Adaptability and imaginativeness are the establishments of all the preparation. In the World Wide Web, there are many DIY hydroponics plans.

Here is a rundown of the best hydroponics DIY plans that somebody may make. Such projects include setups at the fledgling, progressed, and proficient stage.

The Passive Bucket Kratky Method

Without a doubt, the Kratky Approach is one of the least difficult hydroponic plans you can dispatch in a couple of hours.

This gadget is ideal for somebody who simply has hydroponics going. A bowl, some rising media, (for example, hydroton, perlite), some net tanks, hydroponic supplements, and pH units are all you require. These are expected to set up a detached gadget (no vitality required) that will work persistently without support for a considerable length of time. You will create green vegs, for example, lettuces, spinach at the start, or organic product plants, for example, tomatoes once you have enough ability.

Simple Bucket Hydroponic System

This is simply one more essential learner hydroponic framework. What you need is a 5-gallon holder, some rising media, for example, coconut or perlite vermiculite, and a blend of supplements.

The framework works by utilizing the rising media to build up a fine movement that moves supplements to the underlying foundations of plants. Perfect for single huge plants, this gadget. You can water the machine physically on the off chance that you need to keep things straightforward.

You may require an additional pail for the tank and a sub siphon and clock for a programmed framework.

Basic Drip System with Buckets

Another passage level choice, this is somewhat more advanced than the above single pail technique. This would all be able to be cobbled along with bits that cost at least under $100.

The underlying structure plans for the development of various pails of four seeds, both took care of by a solitary store. It is an extremely flexible framework to create in the Future.

Given the size of the plants concerned, you ought to change the holder limit and supply. You may utilize huge tanks of 4 gallons or littler barrels.

For this case, you need to join more plants to the blend later, attempt to buy a greater tank.

Aquarium Hydroponics Raft

It's an entirely fun plan to consider going all in the hydroponic condition. It's an ideal method to get your youngsters dependent on the game, as well.

You'll require, as the name suggests, an amphibian fish tank to carry out this responsibility. You may utilize this gadget to create little beans or even solitary large lettuce. Notwithstanding the ordinary supplies, for example, compost, fuel, and vegetables, you'll need a freight boat pontoon made out of froth. Utilizing siphons and vitality, the gadget might be inactive or dynamic.

PVC NFT Hydroponics

You may utilize full 4-inch PVC funnels to construct your home fabricated hydroponic gadget. The plants are placed in this structure in cups that are situated in holders penetrated the channels.

A siphon and supply feed the machine. This is a shut gadget, with the water between the channels and the tank streaming.

This structure is ideal for expanding huge amounts of little plants in a restricted area. Out of 20-40 plants, the straightforward gadget will house anyplace.

This machine can be introduced outside or inside. Developing lights are, obviously, essential if they are inside.

The arrangement of hydroponics utilized in this plant is called NFT. It is a superb plan to raise seedlings, for example, tomatoes.

Hydroponic Grow Box

This DIY program is an extremely vigorous system and can move a considerable amount around. It tends to be rendered utilizing any capacity tub or canister of any kind. It will be fixed with a lock.

The system uses PVC tubing, a sub-generator, and sprinkler sets out toward the water system to furnish the plants with supplements and water.

The plants are held pressed with a specific rising medium in net cups. The case's top should hold certain net cups.

Edge Hydroponic System

The hydroponic edge configuration is extremely near the hydroponic gadget worked of PVC. It utilizes similar ideas concentrated on NFT to take care of the plants with supplements and water.

The differentiation here is that the verticality has expanded. By including new layers of various statures of PVC pipes, you can develop more plants in a similar space.

This would raise the measure of tubing required, as will the complexity of the siphoning strategy.

This particular plan houses a wooden rack outline lodging the PVC tubing. With this gadget, you will develop herbs and plants, for example, strawberries and tomatoes.

Vertical Window Farm

A remarkable thought that takes care of the lighting issue while giving a captivating window show to the outside world too.

The methodology involves keeping plants in a vertical rack framework with compartments. Reused jugs of water shape extraordinary compartments.

A system of funnels/tubes for giving the plants supplements from the store. Characteristic daylight of need offers light—perfect for flavors, spinach, tomatoes, and chard.

Hydroponic Rain Tower Garden

It is another hydroponic vertical structure, which utilizes a pinnacle system. You can construct the whole framework for about $500.

The pinnacle is made utilizing a fence post. The arrangement is versatile for developing inside and outside.

In breaks cut into the post, the plants are housed in net cups, which are dispersed uniformly over the post length.

For moving water to the pinnacle, a generator is required. The water streams down within, start to finish, arriving at each plant.

Basic Desktop Hydroponic System

The name tells everything. This is an extremely modest technique for hydroponics, which can be put around your work area.

The structure is perfect for a little plant, similar to lettuce or a herb. This is ideal for apprentices who have little space to extend.

The plan involves utilizing a half-gallon can as the key tub, or even an espresso pot. The plant, similar to shake yarn, is housed in a net cup with a rising substrate.

A minuscule bubbler is the costliest segment of this framework.

Mason Jar Kratky Method for Hydroponics

It is a low-upkeep framework with no force or motors included. From the program verbally expressed above, you have run into the Kratky framework. However, rather than the holder, this one uses Mason's container.

This machine does exclude any unique devices or equipment. Numerous parts are open promptly in family units.

Not surprisingly, the plants are kept by net cups. This is then contained inside the covers of the Mason container.

The net cups can be made custom made with plastic cups that fit into the bricklayer containers 'mouth. The pots are pressed with the supplement arrangement, so the underlying foundations of the plant will grow inside it.

Dutch Bucket Hydroponics

Dutch basins are additionally delegated cans BATO. They are extraordinarily adaptable tanks of various sizes that can be found in hydroponic frameworks.

You may likewise give a manual water system strategy, where the compost arrangement is added to the plants quite often.

Or on the other hand, you can utilize tubing, engines, and PVC pipes for a brisk recycling gadget. Everything that is required to render a programmed gadget is an essential clock.

This developing strategy might be utilized in plants of various sizes. An entire basin might be given to the bigger plants, while numerous littler herbs might be housed in a similar can.

You may grow a Dutch container framework inside or outside in a nursery/porches, contingent upon the size of the gadget.

Profound Water Culture Hydroponics

This framework is great on the off chance that you decide to develop things like tomatoes and lettuce inside. Cultivators typically utilize a dark plastic stockpiling box as the essential supplement arrangement bottle is lovely.

All through this strategy, from two to eight plants might be developed all over, contingent upon the size of the fenced-in area.

The main different segments expected to siphon in oxygen into the supplement arrangement are a bubbler and some air hoses.

The plants might be placed in net holders; the lights grow under LEDs.

Trickle Water Hydroponics

Trickle frameworks might be fundamental or muddled, because of the spending plan and details.

You ought to forego the siphons in an uninvolved gadget, and use gravity to convey the supplement answer for the plants. This should require some inventive nursery and repository situating.

So you can just utilize a submarine siphon, and a dainty tubing system to flexibly the plants with the supplement arrangement is low.

For trickle frameworks, a developing medium is generally preferred. Coir and perlite-vermiculite are regular decisions.

Ebb Flow System

This is another generally reasonable, DIY gadget that utilizes a capacity plate or tote to house the entire through the procedure.

The ebb-stream strategy involves developing plants in a fluid, at that point at determined occasions filling the fluid with a supplement answer for a couple of moments. It's an occasionally named system of flood-channel.

For programmed movement, this framework would require a siphon just as a clock.

Stackable Hydroponics

Stackable growers are extremely basic for growing a huge amount of plants in the constrained room in restricted nurseries. However, for hydroponics, such heaping gadgets may likewise be utilized.

In any case, at the lower stages, you'll have to figure in the inconsistent move through the plants. Therefore, stacking is certainly not an extremely powerful hydroponics gadget.

However, the investigation is consistently advantageous, regardless of numerous plants requiring changing water and supplement needs.

Natively constructed DIY Hydroponics is considered as both science and craftsmanship.

You may construct imaginative game plans that yield rich improvement as well as wind up looking tastefully satisfying.

Your innovativeness is as far as possible, and obviously, the essential worry to get enough supplements for your plants.

Chapter 13: Frequently Asked Questions

Here's a list of some of the frequently asked questions that I haven't already covered (examples of what I've already covered are the advantages and disadvantages of hydroponics, as well as how it works).

Is Hydroponic Gardening Organic?

This question has no black and white answer. By nature, the nutrients that you feed your plants in hydroponic gardening are synthetic and made of chemicals. Due to this, hydroponic gardening cannot generally be considered organic. Organic farming refers to farming practices that include the cycling of resources, promoting an ecological balance, and conserving biodiversity, which are all different kinds of life on Earth.

Legally in the U.S., organic certification can be extended to crops that are not grown in soil. There are ways in which to ensure that these farms are ecologically sound by merely mimicking nature using high-grade tech— some systems even create a miniature ecosystem by incorporating fish tanks strung together with the plants. Hydroponics already reduces the use of water and energy, so the rest comes down to how you run your system. You can choose to use organic fertilizers and nutrients, organic alternatives to pesticides, natural methods of pest control, and even natural insects themselves such as bees and butterflies that keep the pests away from your crops if you have an open-air system.

Can I Create My Organic Nutrients?

Essentially, whether or not your garden is organic depends on you. You can create organic nutrients for your plants, providing them with what's known as a "compost tea." There are places where you can purchase organic nutrients, but they tend to be pricier than regular nutrients.

Below are two different methods of creating your organic mixture.

1.   The first mixture is known as an organic tea, made entirely from scratch by you, and will require the following products:

- **Compost and/or worm castings**
- **A colander**
- **A large bowl**
- **A large bucket**
- **A cheesecloth**
- **A mixing spoon**

Fill one of the buckets about halfway full with compost and/or worm castings. Everything you use needs to be broken down until it's brown and crumbly, kind of like dirt.

Next, add water to the mix until the bucket is almost full—at least enough that stirring won't cause any of the mixture to spill over the rim. Once you're done stirring, it will need to sit for a minimum of 24 hours. Before you use it, the water will darken to a deep brown, and only then should it be used.

At this point, you'll bring in the cheesecloth and colander. Layer the colander with the cheesecloth and then set it over the empty bucket. The next step is to strain the compost mixture through the colander like a sift. Ensure that there are no major lumps left as they can cause your hydroponic system to fail by clogging the pumps. Repeat the process of pouring the mixture through the colander until there are no solids left.

This liquid will now be used to fill the reservoir instead of the regular chemically-created additives available. You should replace it one to two times per week. If your garden looks like it needs more nutrients, this is an indicator that it's time to replace the liquid in the reservoir and can mean that you need to replace it more often. Some of the signs of nutrient deficiencies in plants include yellow leaves, brown spots, and/or other strange colors that aren't considered ordinary for the particular species.

2.   The second method can be made using commercial products:

- **Water-soluble organic fertilizer**
- **Epsom salts**
- **A measuring spoon**
- **A large bucket**

You'll need to measure out the amount of water that you need for your hydroponic system in gallons. You can either pour this water directly into the reservoir or you can pour it into the bucket.

For each gallon of water, add two teaspoons of fertilizer. Next, add one teaspoon of Epsom salts per gallon of water to the mix.

Lastly, mix it all until everything is completely dissolved. You'll have to replace this liquid at least once a week and more if the plants look nutrient-deprived.

Hydroponics Garden Secret

Is There a Difference Between Organic and Inorganic?

Chemically, there is a difference, but the truth is that the measure should be made with your plants in mind. They won't complain. To them, the nutrients are pretty much the same on a molecular level.

A lot of organic fertilizers require symbiotic fungi and bacteria—which is to say, they form a relationship in which both the plant and the bacteria and/or fungi benefit. What this means is that the bacteria and fungi break down the fertilizer before you can use it, while the inorganic varieties can generally be used immediately. There is a concern that organic fertilizers are also more likely to build up sludge in the reservoir, which can be an additional effort to clean.

Whatever you do, never use hydrogen peroxide with your organic nutrients. Some people use this as a method of ensuring that the reservoir is practically self-cleaning. It's not safe and kills off all the fungi and bacteria that the fertilizer requires to be active, which can, in turn, actually cause more buildup.

How Should I Care for My Nutrient Solution?

You can aerate the nutrient solution now and then, ensuring that it is covered by light and the room is well-ventilated, to improve the health of your garden and prevent any bacterial infections. You may find, particularly if you're using organic solutions, that your solution lasts longer if aerated. It guards against stagnation.

Keep your solution at around 65-70°F for the best growth. You may want a heater for dark periods to prevent the solution from causing your plants to go into shock. In the same vein, you'll want to ensure it doesn't exceed the recommended temperature to prevent your reservoir from becoming a breeding ground for bacterial and fungi infections that could harm your garden.

What Are the Common Things to Look out for in Terms of Plant Health?

There are several things that plants can do that could be a cause for concern, so we'll cover each of those here:

- Plants dying is the biggest worry, but before you can resolve the issue, you need to be able to identify the root cause (see what I did there?). You'll need to eliminate caregiving faux pas, such as dehydration, excessive heat, and broken stems as causes.
  - ✓ If it's not any of the above, it may be a root disease such as Pythium, which is the most common reason why plants "suddenly" die (in actuality, the plant will have been suffering for some time and there may have been a loss of yield before its death). Temperature control is important to prevent these from occurring. If you know your reservoir is prone to temperature rises, you can use a nutrient conditioner that prevents the pathogens of root diseases from taking hold.
- Leaves may yellow and there are multiple causes (and you can use your EC/pH meters to monitor and control this):
  - ✓ If it's especially on older and lower leaves, nitrogen deficiency is the cause of this problem, so the easiest way to correct it would be to add nitrogen when you feed the plants. You can mix worm castings and pine tree oil for safe methods.
  - ✓ Sometimes, newer leaves may yellow, which is probably due to a micronutrient blockage. It's generally phosphorus or potassium toxicity or unbalanced pH levels at fault. Get some pH-balanced

water and flush out the medium you use to grow before watering it with a new, quality nutrient solution.

✓ An alternate cause to newer leaves yellowing may be as simple as your lamps being too close to the leaves, which can result in yellow or brown hues. Try moving the bulbs away.

✓ Lastly, you can also overpower your plants by overwatering them, and this can cause yellowing. If you're overwatering, it can result in a lack of oxygen. Essentially, you'll be drowning and starving your plants.

- The tips of your plants can burn if too much food is in your reservoir or there is a deficiency (the latter occurs rarely if you use EC/pH meters). The nutrient solution builds up, including a buildup of salt, which burns the plants much like too much salt would burn our mouths. Flushing the system will help prevent and resolve the issue.

- Plants can become stretchy. This takes up space and hinders growth production. If plants are far from light or competing with other plants for light, the airflow in your garden is poor, or the humidity is higher than it should be, this can happen.

Should I Prune the Leaves Away?

Removing large leaves could be more harmful than anything else to certain plants. They take a long time to develop their leaves, so cutting them could stunt development. Always be careful to avoid the larger leaves for good measure, but feel free to further research trimming techniques per the specific plant you're growing.

What Is That Sludge and How Do I Remove It?

Speaking of sludge—yes, there can be a buildup similar to the scum found in dirty fish tanks, for the same reason. It could be bacteria, fungi, algae, or any combination thereof. The problem with this buildup, apart from being downright gross, is that these organisms can take all the oxygen and nutrients from your reservoir, which leaves nothing for your garden. They can also block and clog your pumps, drippers, and nozzles. In short, they can be gardening nightmares.

Rather than remove the buildup after it's already formed, you should be working on preventing it from forming at all. The growth of these organisms is usually caused by higher room temperatures and light entering the reservoir. Therefore, the best way to prevent this from happening is by ensuring no light enters the reservoir and it is kept cool.

You can use a reservoir cooler, or keep the room cool, and cover it with a lid or black plastic to keep the light from entering. Cleaning your reservoir every time you change it will also help prevent the buildup. There are several suitable food-grade cleansers to use, and in place of hydrogen peroxide, vinegar may be used as an organic cleanser.

If at any point, having completed all of the above steps, you are still finding algae growing in your reservoir, you should check your airline to make sure there is no growth there. It will almost only happen if you use transparent airlines because they allow light in. Purchasing and using non-transparent airlines will help prevent this from happening, as will covering the airline with colored tape.

How Often Should I Clean out My Reservoir?

The amount of time necessary to empty and replace the nutrient solution in your reservoir isn't different depending on whether you go "organic" or "chemical." The recommended amount of time is five to seven days. A lot of people use their EC/TDS meters to measure the nutrient levels of their plants, but the problem with this is that the meters can only measure the salt levels, rather than the precise nutrients.

The only way to ensure your nutrient levels are giving your plants what they need consistently is to empty the reservoir and replace your nutrient solution with quality fertilizers every week. If there are any nutrients unused by your garden, they can build up. This could be toxic.

Hydroponics Garden Secret

Chapter 14: More Hydroponic Plants

Valerian

Valerian is an herbaceous plant that originates in central Europe and Asia but is now widespread also in western Europe and North America. The valerian develops very broadly and can reach a height of one and a half meters. The rhizome of the valerian plant is composed of many roots that are characterized by an unpleasant smell.

The typical environment of the valerian is the areas rich in humidity, the margins of the courses of the rivers, woods, etc... However, we can cultivate it very well even in our gardens when it has no particular needs. The optimal climate for the cultivation of valerian is the temperate one, however, this plant can withstand even temperatures of fifteen degrees below zero; likes sun exposure but also semi-shaded.

Valerian is multiplied by seed, by the division of the rhizome or tuft. Before proceeding with sowing, the soil will be worked deeply. If seed multiplication is chosen, it will be done during the spring period starting from the seedbed; this operation takes a long time because the valerian has a very slow development.

Borage

Borage alias cucumber. Borage has a taste of fresh green cucumber, which makes it excellent in salads or on spreads. In medicine, the seeds of the plant or the borage oil derived from it are used mainly for skin complaints.

Angelica

The angelica is one of the few medicinal plants that are native to northern Europe and from the north - Greenland, and Iceland - by planting in the medieval monastery gardens in the 14th century. Central Europe has become their habitat. For about 500 years, the effects of this magnificent and stately plant in herbal books are described. The spectrum ranges from folk medicine to modern phytotherapy, from the protection against a plague disease to the magenta therapeutic. Its manifold application in the past has brought the angelica also many more names, so we find for them names such as butterbur, theraminwurz, brustwurz, heiliggeistwurz, according to their preferred use. In the alpine region, we often find the wild angelica or waldengelwurz - Angelica Sylvestris.

Although it also reaches a height of more than one meter and is thus an attractive Umbelliferae in the landscape From these effects, the following fields of application for this aromatic amarum (bitter agent) can be derived: loss of appetite can thus be favorably influenced; if dyspeptic symptoms and mild gastrointestinal spasms are present, these can be well removed with preparations from the root of the angelica. Often, feelings of fullness and bloating are triggered by stressful situations that also respond well to this medicinal plant. In addition to the medicinal use of the angelica root, it is also processed in herb schnapps, liqueurs, and other digestive (digestive preparations); but also, the seasoning of sauces, salads, and other foods is the tart aroma of angelica. The flower stems of the plant are used for candying and thus form a sweet variation in Austrian pastry art.

Strawberries

Hydroponics technical system that allows the greenhouse cultivation of fruit and vegetables on a sluggish substrate or not, by optimally managing the elements that determine the quality of the plants and the product: temperature, irrigation, light, etc.

The hydroponics in general and the strawberry, in particular, allows to the improvement of all the elements responsible for the quality of the plant and the final product, through higher production and higher quality, u the solution to the problems arising from the cultural soil (dirt, slowness, fungi, mold...) And the standardization of production. Hydroponics strawberries can also be adopted for smaller plants, such as home, thanks to the cost rather than content and ease of installation.

In the fruit and vegetable sector, the introduction of strawberry technology

was favored by specific structural and ecological conditions of this crop: in recent years, the cultivation of strawberries also encountered rapid development, moving from classical cultivation in open land cultivation land substrate and especially bags of peat.

With hydroponics, strawberries are constantly kept in optimal nutritional conditions, because the techniques used guarantee phytosanitary conditions best and cleanest product. The result is higher quality strawberries, with a better look, a consistent size, inherent properties better to endure (less crude fiber content a higher percentage of sugar fats, vitamins, a higher density), lower availability, and increased capacity of long-distance transport.

Cultivated strawberries are hydroponically protected by the adoption of different types of tunnels, depending on the investment cost and depreciation, openings have been tested and afford by the side or side and are usually made of plastic films each takes an average of 3-4 years, with average brightness and good thermal insulation properties. Grow bags can be placed in a set of files of pedestals or hung in the height of the structure, which can be useful to receive the product in the palms of individual farmers. Strawberry plants are planted in plastic bags (from 4 to 6 per bag) of 10-12 liters per lot, with sizes of 20-25 cm wide 35-40 cm

Hydroponics Garden Secret

long. The contents of the bags are usually made of white peat and pear in a variable portion.

However, there are many types of hydroponics for the production of strawberries that reach each other for how the water reaches the roots of the plant.

Cucumbers

Hydroculture for cucumbers with your own hands will be very welcome in the economy if you want to get a good harvest of this vegetable quickly. Cucumbers are climbers, so it is better in small hydroponics to sow them along the wall of the pallet, and after the shoots appear, bind them to the installed at an angle stops. This method helps breeders looking for a way to grow cucumbers quickly. Such placement of cucumbers does not disturb other plants that may also be in this range, and the bound cucumbers eventually produce fruits of much higher quality. The optimal growth of cucumbers contributes to the bright day up to 14 hours.

Melons

Melons probably come from the subtropical regions of Asia and have been cultivated for millennia. As their botanical name suggests Cucumis melo, they are related to the cucumbers. The Cucumis melo is distributed as sugar or honeydew melon, cantaloupe melon, and nettle melon. The watermelon (Citrullus lanatus) belongs to a different genus. Cantaloupe melons are usually recognized by their firm orange flesh. The shell is hard, scaly, and traversed by longitudinal grooves.

The variety of 'Charentais' is considered precocious. Depending on the variety, honeydew melons have a smooth or ribbed yellow to greenish skin. Inside they are yellowish to white or orange. Net melons can be recognized by the net pattern of the shell. The flesh is green to white or salmon-colored. The fruits of the variety 'hale's best jumbo' can weigh up to two kilograms. Melons germinate at temperatures between 20 and 30 degrees Celsius. Therefore, we recommend that you prefer plants in warm conditions. In April, you can sow the seeds one to two centimeters deep and place them on a warm, sunny windowsill. Our tip: if you sow in small pots, you do not need to pimp them. The plants are sensitive to

127

cold. Therefore, it is best to plant them in the second half of May or early June - ideally in the greenhouse. The distance between the melon plants should be 80 by 80 centimeters.

Location and care

Melons need a lot of heat. The more sun and heat they get, the better the fruits will grow, and the sweeter and more aromatic they become. Some varieties thrive well in partial shade, as long as it is warm enough.

They also make some demands on the ground. He should be relaxed and nutritious. The best way is to prepare the bed of compost and give them some

slow-release fertilizer in the planting hole. Additional fertilizers during the summer need strong-consuming plants. Also, you should always pour it sufficiently.

For melons to plant many fruits, it is recommended to cut them: cap the main shoot after the fourth or fifth leaf so that its branches. Repeat the procedure for the side shoots after four to eight leaves. The following shoots then form the flowers and later the fruits.

You can pull melons on trellises or spread them on the ground. Then put a board under the fruit, so they do not rot.

Melons are considered to be sensitive to fungal diseases such as fusarium wilt. They can also be attacked by powdery mildew and downy mildew.

Harvest and use of melons

Depending on the sowing season and season melons mature from august. Whether you can harvest them, you will recognize them by their color and their sweet scent. For some varieties, the stalk dries. It is best to harvest the melons quickly by separating them from the plant with a sharp knife. Overripe fruits do not taste that good anymore.

You can eat melons in the summer just like that. You can also use them for salads, desserts, and cold drinks. Since they are not very durable, you eat them right away.

Tomatoes

Hydroponic seedlings, including tomatoes, are grown in small pots floating or suspended over water so that the tomato roots absorb the necessary amount of nutrient-rich water necessary for the tomatoes or other hydroponic plants to grow. An unsinkable support system must first be built or purchased to plant and grow using the hydroponic method.

Instructions

Purchase hydroponic plant trays for growing tomatoes. Trays with larger holes are used to better support adult tomato plants (remember, if you want to grow the tomatoes completely in the hydroponic beds or pimp them in a garden or pot during the warm growing season).

Use a cutter to cut larger holes in hydroponic plant trays with holes for adult tomato plants too small. Be careful not to let the lower ends taper conically to allow the root system to fall through to provide better watering results.

Purchase or build a waterbed to place the trays. Build the beds of wooden frames on the inside covered with a single solid sheet of plastic.

Fill the plant tray holes halfway down the ground and drop a tomato seed into each hole. Cover the seeds, fill the tray with holes, and then place them in the waterbeds, where the trays remain over water at the surface of the water, with only enough of the tray so that the tomato plant roots can absorb the necessary amount of water.

Conclusion

Hydroponic cultivating is equivalent to normal planting except if there is no wreckage by any means. Indoor hydroponic cultivating has no dirt. Have you at any point seen the well known Babylon Hanging Gardens? This is one of the world's Seven Wonders and is most likely the soonest proof of our indoor hydroponic planting in humanity's history.

Not many individuals presently have the assets to deliver something as rich as this natural marvel, however, in a hydroponic nursery, we can develop our minibar. It is equivalent to a customary nursery, yet hydroponic because all plants are developed with water, light, and air.

That is bogus. That is correct. There is no requirement for soil. This is actually what indoor hydroponic cultivating is about. Developing in a hydroponic nursery, your preferred products of the soil are the most recent prevailing fashion among plant specialists. All that you need and on the off chance that you truly need to go to the nearby lake and nursery shop and hydroponic bundles. Or then again you test all the great may make your own.

Suggestion to an amateur, be that as it may, is to get one of the hydroponic units. Numerous individuals utilize one of the two famous hydroponic units: a hydroponic rhythmic movement pack or a hydroponic profound culture Pack. These future basic hydroponic bundles all your hydroponic nursery needs to begin. On the off chance that you need to expand your hydroponic nursery, you will most likely need to purchase extra lights and increasingly supplement arrangements. In any case, it's a wise interest over the long haul.

Logical examinations show that hydroponic nursery merchandise is lighter, juicier, and more nutritious than store buys. The extra reward is that there are no weed gives that outside nurseries typically face. In a hydroponic nursery, there are not many irritations. This, thus, implies unsafe and risky pesticides and bug sprays are not required. Another extraordinary preferred position is that you can develop your preferred leafy foods during the time with hydroponic units. Better believe it! Amazing! How cool this is! You could at whatever season develop your food, shield your family from hurtful synthetics, and make the most of your preferred nourishments.

Hydroponic indoor planting is an awesome diversion. There is essentially no messiness, no added substances, and numerous advantages can be found in the eye. You grow a nursery that you appreciate and maintain a strategic distance from all the drawbacks and cerebral pains that generally accompany cultivating. Go out, at that point, if you need to take a stab at something new. Take a portion of your mates, go to the store and buy hydroponic packs and make your hydroponic nursery.

In addition to the fact that hydroponics allows for quick, proficient, financially savvy developing conditions, however, it is a way to develop products where it in any case couldn't develop. On account of creative water system frameworks and the utilization of different developing media, puts that have lacking soil organization can develop new products.

Hydroponics additionally gives a developing answer for places that have almost no space for business developing terrains. It has even been effectively tried in space. Hydroponics is certifiably not another idea yet has made some amazing progress since antiquated occasions and continues pushing ahead by a wide margin with new techniques being presented en route.

Hydroponics Garden Secret

It's anything but a hard idea to handle and a few strategies are extremely simple to learn. There are instant packs that one can purchase and gather for each kind of framework. Yet, they are generally equipped for being natively constructed with materials found around the home.

Hydroponics is an incredible method to show youngsters the delight of cultivating without the chaos of soil and as the plants develop moderately rapidly it holds their consideration better than typical cultivating does.